INTRODUCTION TO CHRISTIAN WORSHIP

GRAMMAR, THEOLOGY, & PRACTICE

STEVEN D. BRUNS

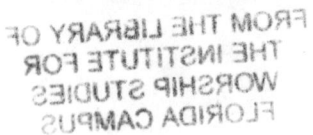

Introduction to Christian Worship: Grammar, Theology, and Practice

The General Board of Higher Education and Ministry leads and serves The United Methodist Church in the recruitment, preparation, nurture, education, and support of Christian leaders—lay and clergy—for the work of making disciples of Jesus Christ for the transformation of the world. Its vision is that a new generation of Christian leaders will commit boldly to Jesus Christ and be characterized by intellectual excellence, moral integrity, spiritual courage, and holiness of heart and life. The General Board of Higher Education and Ministry of The United Methodist Church serves as an advocate for the intellectual life of the church. The Board's mission embodies the Wesleyan tradition of commitment to the education of laypersons and ordained persons by providing access to higher education for all persons.

Wesley's Foundery Books is named for the abandoned foundery that early followers of John Wesley transformed, which later became the cradle of London's Methodist movement.

Introduction to Christian Worship: Grammar, Theology, and Practice

Copyright 2019 by Wesley's Foundery Books

Wesley's Foundery Books is an imprint of the General Board of Higher Education and Ministry, The United Methodist Church. All rights reserved.

No part of this book may be reproduced in any form whatsoever, print or electronic, without written permission, except in the case of brief quotations embodied in critical articles or reviews. For information regarding rights and permissions, contact the Publisher, General Board of Higher Education and Ministry, PO Box 340007, Nashville, TN 37203-0007; phone 615-340-7393; fax 615-340-7048. Visit our website at www.gbhem.org.

All web addresses were correct and operational at the time of publication.

ISBN 978-1-945935-40-4

Unless otherwise indicated, Scripture quotations are taken from the New Revised Standard Version Bible, copyright © 1989 the Division of Christian Education of the National Council of the Churches of Christ in the United States of America. Used by permission. All rights reserved.

Scripture quotations marked KJV are taken from The Authorized (King James) Version. Rights in the Authorized Version in the United Kingdom are vested in the Crown. Reproduced by permission of the Crown's patentee, Cambridge University Press.

Extracts from The Book of Common Prayer, the rights in which are vested in the Crown, are reproduced by permission of the Crown's patentee, Cambridge University Press.

19 20 21 22 23 24 25 26 27 28—10 9 8 7 6 5 4 3 2 1

Manufactured in the United States of America

CONTENTS

Introduction 1
1 The Priesthood of All Believers 13
2 The Theology of Ordination 29
3 Sacred Spaces 49
4 The Order of Worship 65
5 The Church Year 99
6 Sacraments 113
7 The Sacrament of Baptism 121
8 The Sacrament of Holy Communion 139
9 Music in Worship 157
10 Other Services 169
11 Practicalities 181
Conclusion 195
Appendix A: Worship Service Worksheet 199
Appendix B: Prayer Services 203
Appendix C: The Covenant Renewal Service 211
Appendix D: Lectionary 217
Index 229

INTRODUCTION

On the first Pentecost after the resurrection of Jesus, the church grew exponentially. Before that morning, according to the Book of Acts, 120 disciples followed Jesus as Messiah. After the descent of the Holy Spirit and Peter's sermon, 3,000 people converted and joined the church. That was a 2,600 percent increase after one message! Jesus did say that his followers would do greater works than he did, and this was one of them. He fed 5,000 people, and they just went home. Peter told a crowd that they had rejected the Messiah and handed him over to be killed, and 3,000 converted.

As amazing as this mass conversion was, it did pose a problem for the fledgling community. The original group of disciples in the upper room knew Jesus. Many of them had spent the entire three-year ministry with him, traveling around Galilee and Judea. They heard his teaching, and they knew his heart. Now that group was outnumbered twenty-five to one. How would they teach so many new people what it means to follow Jesus? How would they ensure these new people would comprehend the uniqueness of this new movement? How would the disciples prevent their group from being swallowed up by the massive wave of new converts with different backgrounds and opinions? The disciples taught these new converts how to worship.

With such a huge influx of new believers, people who may have heard of Jesus and knew something of his ministry but did not follow him directly or participate in the life of his followers, the church needed to do something for them. Four things stood out to the older members as the most important aspects of their life together to teach and form these new members. "They devoted themselves to the apostles' teaching and fellowship, to the breaking of bread and the prayers" (Acts 2:42). These are the four elements that have served as the model of worship for the nearly two thousand years that have followed. The forms have changed, but these four elements, to a greater or lesser extent, have remained a constant in the worship practice of the church.

Lex Orandi, Lex Credendi

The reason these four elements of worship were seen as the most essential things to teach new converts was because the earliest Christians understood the principle later codified in the Latin phrase *lex orandi, lex credendi*. This means "the law of prayer is the law of belief" or "the rule of prayer is the rule of belief." In other words, how people worship forms what they believe, and in turn what they believe informs how they worship. Since there was no New Testament yet, the only way to communicate the faith in such a way as to ensure the same faith was being shared and experienced everywhere was to teach people how to worship. By using these four elements to greater or lesser degrees, the church taught people who the God is who acted in Jesus Christ and what their relationship was to this God.

Whether or not people have ever heard of this Latin phrase today, the principle still holds true. What people believe about God shapes how they worship, and how they worship forms what they believe about God. From liturgical forms of worship to Pentecostal passion, the way people worship shapes their understanding of who God is. Therefore, it is vital for the church to understand what it does in worship and why. This is also why it is essential to be able to comprehend and communicate what worship is to congregation members. If the earliest Christians, under the Holy Spirit's guidance, thought worship was the most important thing to teach a very large group of converts, perhaps it is something Christians today should be taught.

INTRODUCTION

Apostolic Teaching

The apostles' teaching has served as the basis of our understanding of who Jesus is and what he has done. In these first days of the church, this teaching was new commentary on the Scriptures (what we now call the Old Testament) and the apostles' remembrances of Jesus's teaching and preaching. The Bible we have today is a direct product and witness of that teaching itself, as the books of the New Testament were either written by apostles or by those who knew them and preserved their teachings. Jesus commissioned the apostles to be his "witnesses in Jerusalem, in all Judea and Samaria, and to the ends of the earth" (Acts 1:8) and to "make disciples of all nations, baptizing them in the name of the Father and of the Son and of the Holy Spirit, and teaching them to obey everything that I have commanded you" (Matthew 28:19-20). Given this injunction to pass on and teach Jesus's message to the whole world, it is only logical that their teaching would be an integral part of the life of the new church.

This teaching comprised the good news, or the gospel, namely, that God had decisively acted in history in Jesus Christ to reconcile humanity to God. It incorporated the entire narrative of Jesus's birth, life, crucifixion, resurrection, and ascension as the continuation and fulfillment of the story of Israel. It was seen as the solution to the fall of humanity and not just redemption, but rather, the inauguration of a whole new creation. This is how, within the context of worship, the new converts were taught about who this God was that they were worshiping. It was how they were brought into a deeper understanding of who they were and who they were becoming.

As this teaching spread to new people and new communities, it was almost a foregone conclusion that there would be different interpretations and understandings. Even within the biblical picture of the church there were already instances where the community had to make a decision or take a stand against a false teaching. One prime example concerned the issue of circumcision. The debate over whether or not

Gentiles had to become Jews to be redeemed by the Jewish Messiah was hotly contested, as a cursory reading of Galatians reveals. On top of this, there was also the danger of an encroaching proto-Gnosticism that is argued against in John's epistles and Jude. The apostolic teaching quickly took on the aspect of not only transmitting what the apostles taught, but also attempting to preserve its original understanding by "contend[ing] for the faith that was once for all entrusted to the saints" (Jude 3).

The first century drew to a close but the complex questions concerning the good news remained. Many and varied voices competed for the right to claim they were championing the faith. As each new perspective was made public, the church had to decide to accept or reject that perspective, trusting fully that it was the Holy Spirit, promised by Jesus, that would "teach [them] everything, and remind [them] of all that [he had] said to [them . . . and] guide [them] into all the truth" (John 14:26; 16:13). This was the age of the great theological debates that gave the church the seven ecumenical councils, the Nicene Creed, the Symbol of Chalcedon, and what we consider the historically orthodox understanding of the church today. And it is this teaching that is still an essential portion of worship to this day.

The Fellowship

The fellowship, in a real way, was the gathering together and community of those believers. It was their lives intertwined with one another so that a new family was founded, one whose Father is God and whose family members were siblings of Christ (Luke 8:19-21). It is in this frame of reference that Paul could say, "It is that very Spirit bearing witness with our spirit that we are children of God, and if children, then heirs, heirs of God and fellow heirs with Christ" (Romans 8:16-17).

This understanding of fellowship is also the basis for the understanding of the church as the body of Christ (1 Corinthians 12:12-31), the twelve tribes (James 1:1), and the temple of God (1 Peter 2:4-8).

These descriptions of the church show that there is more to it than a mere collection of individuals. There is more to the nature of the church than a group of people with similar morals and beliefs. In fact, the very existence of a church presupposes that there is something to be gained in community and fellowship. Jesus could have sent his apostles out to proclaim the gospel message, convert individuals, and move on to the next place without setting up actual congregations in which these new Christians could meet and worship. Instead, he gathered together a group of people into a new community and sent them out to create more communities that are collectively called "the church."

When Jesus made his profound statement concerning his mission, he said, "On this rock I will build my church, and the gates of Hades will not prevail against it" (Matthew 16:18). It is the church that will have the victory, not individual believers. There is something powerful in being in community with Christians, which is why this was one of the four essential elements of worship for the church. This understanding of the nature of the church leaves little room for the person who decides that he or she better encounters God apart from a worship service and would rather be out in nature, on the golf course, listening to music, in solitary prayer, or in any other isolated setting. John Wesley railed against this idea of individualized Christianity when he wrote, "Solitary religion is not to be found there. 'Holy Solitaries' is a phrase no more consistent with the gospel than holy adulterers. The gospel of Christ knows no religion, but social; no holiness but social holiness."[1]

The Breaking of Bread

In Holy Communion the church has an opportunity to meet and receive God anew. Throughout the last approximately thirteen hundred years of history, Christians have debated exactly how God meets

---

[1] John Wesley, "Hymns and Sacred Poems" (1739), in The Works of John Wesley, Bicentennial ed., ed. Richard P. Heitzenrater (Nashville: Abingdon, 2005), 13.39. Hereinafter, Works.

INTRODUCTION

people in the Eucharist. The honest answer is that no one knows how it happens, but it is known that in the Lord's Supper, God is present. This begs the question, though, what is so special about this element of worship that it can be known that God is decidedly present? What is it, specifically?

Part of the answer concerning the breaking of bread can be found in the meaning behind its many names. *Breaking of bread* conveys a simple act of sharing among one another as Christians. It also is a reminder that Jesus used the broken bread to show us his suffering. Paul recorded Jesus's words as such in 1 Corinthians 11:24, "Take, eat: this is my body which is broken for you" (KJV). *The Lord's Table* is a reminder that it is God's table to which the church is invited, not the church's table at which God is invoked. This is a profound demonstration of grace in that Christ calls his people to himself, not to some ritual that the people expect him to bless. *The Lord's Supper* is a reminder that this was a meal shared among friends, a teacher, and his disciples. It is still such a meal for sustenance as disciples of the Teacher. *Holy Communion* explicitly states that what happens during this element of worship is, in fact, holy. It is of God. It is from God. Therefore, it is holy. In addition, it is a communion with God and with one another as the church partakes of the Communion elements. *The sacrament* shows that there is more happening during this element of worship than can readily be seen. There is a sign, in this case bread and cup, but that sign points to a reality beyond itself, the reality of God's presence among the people. *The Holy Mysteries* is a title that is a reminder not only that what happens in this element of worship is holy, but that its exact nature is unknown. It is mystical and of divine origin, which means no one can ever fully understand what it is. *Eucharist* is actually a Greek word that simply means "thanksgiving." This comes from the gospel account of the event in which Jesus "gave thanks" (Matthew 26:26-29; Mark 14:22-25; Luke 22:14-23) before breaking the bread and giving the cup. In the early church, when this element of worship occurred, the bread was said to be *eucharized*. Eventually the event itself became known as the Eucharist, the Thanksgiving. For all of these reasons, the Lord's Supper was seen as absolutely essential for worship. This will be dealt with more fully in chapters 4 and 8.

The Prayers

Prayer, as a conversation with God, is essential to the Christian life. In fact, all major religions that have a belief in a god or gods have prayer as a part of their belief systems. Prayer is a way of sharing burdens, seeking guidance, petitioning for forgiveness, and requesting action on the part of the self or for another. Prayer is so vital for a living faith and relationship with God that it was one of the only direct requests for teaching that the disciples brought to Jesus. "He [Jesus] was praying in a certain place, and after he had finished, one of his disciples said to him, 'Lord, teach us to pray, as John taught his disciples'" (Luke 11:1).

The prayers that were taught to those new believers after Pentecost certainly included the Lord's Prayer. They may have included other prayers that made their way into many of the letters of the New Testament as affirmations of faith and mini-creeds. Such is the case with Philippians 2:5-11 and specifically Christian interpretations of psalms such as Psalm 110 in Acts 4:25-28. Acts also recorded that the early Christians used the established hours for prayer during the day (Acts 3:1; 10:9, 30; 16:25).

What Is Christian Worship?

If apostolic teaching, fellowship, breaking of bread, and the prayers are elements essential to Christian worship, what do they combine to form? What exactly is Christian worship? This is the next logical question, but it is quite difficult to answer. Unlike other issues in the church, and unlike the first disciples, most congregations do not teach a class in worship. Lack of Bible knowledge? Offer more studies. Flat spiritual life? Offer retreats or prayer seminars. Stewardship problems? Preach a sermon series. Offer a new program. How do Christians worship?

INTRODUCTION

People are expected to learn through osmosis, by simply showing up and doing what everyone else is doing. Given the principle of *lex orandi lex credendi*, the image of God people come to believe may even be adversely affected by not understanding what worship is, what they are doing, or why, especially if the congregation does not have all four elements or emphasizes something else altogether. A congregation could have all four of these elements in worship, completely adhering to the principles outlined earlier, and still not have an appropriate understanding of God or of worship. This is not a guarantee for success; but it is an influential tool for understanding and practicing worship.

Part of the problem with trying to teach people about worship is that there is no real agreement on what the term *worship* really means. Is it the music before the sermon? Is it the whole service? Is it something people attend? Is it something people do? What is Christian worship? While the origin of the English word *worth-ship* (or *weorthscipe*) means "acknowledging something or someone as worthy," this does not help in arriving at the core of what it means for individuals together. There are the different terms the church has used in different times and places to describe worship: service, Mass, Divine Liturgy. Each of these brings more clarity to the question.

Service is used in various forms by Protestants (especially the Wesleyan/Methodist branch) and implies action. It can either be action performed or action received, but it is action nonetheless. *Mass* is used mostly by Roman Catholics and connotes images of sacrifice today, but the term originally meant "sending." The people were sent into the presence of God, their sins were sent away from them, and finally the people were sent into the world. *Divine Liturgy* is used by Eastern and Oriental Orthodox churches and is an interesting term. *Liturgy* is literally "the work of the people." Add *Divine* to that and the term becomes a comingling of God and the people together doing something, the "work."

To try to formulate an answer to the question of what Christian worship is, one can begin to piece together insights from these terms.

INTRODUCTION

Christian worship involves both God and the new covenant people in some sort of action that acknowledges God as worthy. Explaining worship that way, though, is a bit cumbersome and also a dry definition of one of the most important things new converts were to be taught in the earliest days of the church, and it fails to account for the fact that worship has changed lives ever since that first Pentecost.

Instead of trying to define Christian worship, perhaps it would be better to describe it. For worship to be Christian, it must involve the Christian God and Christian people, which is the heart of *lex orandi, lex credendi*. This means that the time spent gathered together must be focused on the Trinity: Father, Son, and Holy Spirit. One of the beautiful descriptions of Christians from the Bible is the body of Christ. In this context, human beings, who have been grafted into Christ and are now a part of his body, are invited to participate in the life of the Trinity. Humans are swept up into the God who is Love. This is a more poetic way to answer the question, *What is Christian worship*? But both descriptions are correct, yet they answer in different ways. Just as the church has used different terms for worship, so too has it described worship differently. And therein is the reason sincerely inquiring Christians are so often left to themselves to try to answer the question. But what if there was a basic language of worship? What if there was a basic grammar for what constitutes Christian worship? The vocabulary may be different; some branches of the church may have larger or smaller, more ancient or modern vocabulary, but the basic structure was the same?

The premise of this book is just that. There is a basic grammar to worship, and grammar tells a story. It is a story of God's people seeking God and of God descending to God's people. "Draw near to God, and he will draw near to you" (James 4:8). These are the key movements in worship that the four elements from Acts 2:42 enable. This story is retold each time the people of God gather for worship. It can take different forms: prayer and Scripture to elevate the people to heavenly places, and the Eucharist, where heaven descends to earth;

INTRODUCTION

sermon exposition to draw people heavenward in thought and conversion as a result when Christ condescends to abide with the contrite of heart; people lost in wonder, love, and praise and the power of the Holy Spirit poured out on the Body. It is the same story of people being lifted to the heavenly realms and God coming to meet them together.

In addition, a basic grammar for worship needs the requisite parts of speech. This book will use this model to give a basic understanding of Christian worship. It will look at the nouns and verbs of worship. Who are the people? What are the places, the things, the ideas? What are the actions of worship? And how do they tell the same story with different vocabulary? At the end of the book, this will be an answer to the question, *What is Christian worship*? While this is a broad Protestant introduction to worship, it will draw from a Wesleyan/Methodist perspective.

One more point needs to be made, though, before the grammar begins. Worship and evangelism are two different things in the life of the church. They can overlap, but they are not one and the same. The basic story retold in worship has God's people moving heavenward as God meets them in the service. Evangelism is driven by the need to share the good news of Christ with those who are not yet part of God's people. In essence, worship is for those inside the church—who are already a part of the Body. Evangelism is for those outside of the church—those not yet Christian. As a result, worship is God-focused, while evangelism is people-focused. Congregations that confuse the two do neither well. Either they do not truly reach new people in the name of Christ, or they do not ascend to the throne of the holy and triune God and come away with a deeper experience of the presence and power of God in their lives.

This does not mean that for an action to be Christian worship it must ignore the people in the world. After all, one of the meanings of Mass was being sent into the world. And it does not mean Christian worship cannot change over time, with different styles or vocabulary. For people to participate in worship, for it to be the work of the

INTRODUCTION

people, it must be in a language they understand. This includes both the spoken word, as the Reformers powerfully reminded the church by bringing worship, song, and Scripture into the vernacular languages once again. It also includes the rhythmic word, styles of music in worship, which is why the church has a cappella chant, organ music, and guitar-driven songs. No matter the form of speech or music, though, the same basic grammar and story, the four elements and two movements, must be told. And that is the point of this book: to give a framework to the grammar of worship.

1

THE PRIESTHOOD OF ALL BELIEVERS

In order to sense worship as something more than a "public cult," it is necessary to see and sense the church as something more than a "society of believers."

—Alexander Schmemann

Worship is about God. The triune God of the Christian message is at the heart of Christian worship. Everything is focused on God, and everything is directed toward God. The three persons of the Trinity are engaged in an eternal dance of unselfish love, a mutual indwelling of each other that is called *perichoresis*. Worship is humanity's participation in that indwelling and being swept up in that dance. Worship is also the work of the people, liturgy. By definition, then, it is necessary for people to participate in worship, and there is no worship without people present and acting. This begs the question, which people? Whose presence and participation are necessary for worship? Clergy? Choir? Trained professionals? Others? To answer this question, it is necessary to look at a brief overview of Christian worship from New Testament times to today. This is because the church has worshiped for about two thousand years. That is a long history filled with examples of what worship is and means and who is involved.

Biblical Texts

Surprisingly, there are not a lot of texts in the New Testament that discuss Christian worship in any detail. Much of the nature of worship was assumed knowledge by all of the various authors of the biblical books. In other words, the Gospel authors, Paul, and the other writers did not take much time and space in their writings to describe something that the community was already doing together regularly. We have a few examples of what happened in early worship from the Bible, but they are mostly hints and tantalizing clues of what New Testament worship was. Here are some of the fundamental texts concerning worship.

John 20	meeting together on Sunday
Acts 2	everyone together, 2:42
Acts 20	meeting together on Sunday
1 Corinthians 11	prophets, tongues, Communion
1 Timothy and Titus	qualifications for bishops, deacons, deaconesses
Revelation 1	worship on the Lord's Day

These texts give the church a broad overview of what worship entailed in the earliest days of the Christian movement. There is very little information contained within these biblical passages that we can use to reconstruct a "New Testament" worship service. This is because the earliest missionaries and apostles spreading the message of Jesus Christ and planting churches verbally taught the church how to worship. What is contained within the Bible is clarifying instructions, side comments that highlight a certain aspect of worship, or corrections of abuses during worship. Readers today are left with incidental comments and corrections to problems. There is no manual for what should or should not be in worship. There is no detailed presentation of what worship ought to resemble or how it should be implemented.

From these passages, a few things can be extrapolated pertaining to worship in these biblical communities.

1. It was important that the new church understood that it was a community of people together, not just individuals. This is obvious from Acts, which emphasizes the reality that followers of Jesus

Christ all met together regularly, to the book of Hebrews, where the injunction to continue to meet together is shared in the face of decreased attendance at the fellowship's gatherings.

2. Many of the gatherings of the entire community for worship were on the first day of the week. This shows that the shift in emphasis for worship from the Sabbath, the seventh day of the week, to the Lord's Day, the first day of the week, was very early in the life of the church. Sunday quickly became the day when the Christian community gathered together to participate in worship.

3. There were various spiritual gifts evident in those gathered communities. Many different people, according to the gifts they had been given by God, participated in worship. Sometimes this participation was for the general edification of the worshiping community, and sometimes it was a distraction. The fact that abuses had to be corrected and excesses had to be curbed shows that the gifts were being used widely and regularly.

4. Baptism and the Lord's Supper were regular events in the life of the community. It is not clear if baptism was celebrated within the context of a worship gathering, but it is clear that the Lord's Supper was present.

5. Leadership emerged within different worshiping communities early. Defined roles for the good of the church arose, such as bishops/presbyters and deacons/deaconesses. These defined roles do not have any responsibilities pertaining to worship within the biblical texts, yet because they very quickly had liturgical roles within the life of the church, it is reasonable to assume that they also had liturgical responsibilities.

Postbiblical and Extra-Biblical Examples

It was actually after the period of the Bible that the earliest discussions of who was involved in worship were recorded. This is for several reasons. First, the earliest generation of Christians was passing away. Members of the second generation were now the elders of the communities, and they needed to remind the newest Christians of what had been taught to them by the original apostles and missionaries. Second, the church gained more visibility and attention from the Roman authorities. This meant that the governors and administrators recorded some of what they discovered concerning this new religion, a religion that might be a threat to the social fabric of Greco-Roman society. Third, in light of this potential new threat, some Christians took it upon themselves to describe what occurred within Christian worship. It is from these early apologists, those Christians who intentionally wrote about the faith for the benefit of those who were not yet a part of the church, that the clearest picture of early Christian worship is found, even though the most detailed of them dates from approximately one hundred years after Peter and Paul were martyred.

One of the earliest recorded examples of the church within the context of worship comes from *The Teaching of the Twelve Apostles*, usually known by its Greek name, the Didache. This text was compiled over a period of time, with some of the earliest layers now believed to have possibly been written around the same time as the Gospel of Mark in the AD 50s–70s. Within this work was a section that described sacramental practice, worship, and the leaders of the community. Worship, according to the Didache, was on the Lord's Day. It was composed of the gathering together as a community to celebrate the Lord's Supper. Interestingly, there were prescribed prayers both during the celebration of the sacrament and after it, even at this early period of time. As well, the sacrament was not to be given to non-Christians, nor were Christian brothers and sisters to come together in worship if they had any divisions between them. Therefore, every Sunday service was required to have a time of confession for the express purpose of reconciling one another together so that they might offer a "pure sacrifice." All the believers participated in this time of confession, and all were involved as a community in the offering of this sacrifice.

The Didache did not record who was responsible for certain leadership aspects of worship; however, there was a curious interchange about four different roles within the church. First, prophets and teachers were equated with "your high priests." This leads to certainly one implication that the Didache was written to believers with Jewish backgrounds. This inference comes from not only the reference to the high priest, but also from the prayers for the Eucharist that are essentially Jewish blessings. The Didache then connected the offerings that were supposed to be given to the temple priesthood, the tithes and first fruits, and now relegated them to the prophets and teachers. Second, the community was commanded to appoint bishops and deacons themselves. These roles were then equated with the roles of prophets and teachers. It would seem by this statement that the titles and roles of leaders within the church at this time were shifting from a gifts-based to a role-based ministry. This is not to say that bishops and deacons were not gifted for the positions they held, but those are not specifically listed as spiritual gifts in the New Testament. Instead, they are leadership roles within the church. Even so, the Didache still only implied who was doing what during a worship service. The service was literally called a *sacrifice*, the prophets and teachers were called high priests, and the bishops and deacons were said to offer the ministry of the prophets and teachers. The implication is that bishops and deacons were taking responsibility for the worship service; but beyond this very strong implication, not much is known for certain.

Potentially contemporaneous with the Didache was a letter known as 1 Clement. It bears this name today because a homily was erroneously attributed to the same author as 2 Clement. Only the numbering of the actual letter is incorrect. There is widespread consensus that it was composed by Clement in Rome around AD 96 and sent to Corinth. Whether or not this Clement was the same one mentioned by Paul

(Philippians 4:3) is unknown. Nevertheless, the letter addressed continuing problems with divisions and factions in the Corinthian church. In the letter, Clement also equated the bishops, alternately called presbyters or elders, and the deacons with the priests and Levites at the temple in Jerusalem.

The next account that gave information about who was involved in worship came from Ignatius of Antioch. Ignatius lived from around AD 30 to 107. He is an interesting figure in church history as he is a transitional figure from the time of the original apostles to the next generation of leadership in the church. Ignatius was bishop in Antioch and was arrested for defiantly holding on to his faith. He was transported from Antioch to Rome and then fed to the lions in the Coliseum. On the way to Rome, he wrote several letters to churches and to one other bishop. Each of these letters is useful and informative on a variety of issues of early church life, but the fact that he felt the need to write to other churches and that these letters were received by them, gives one important, often-overlooked understanding about the early church: it saw itself as one large community, united with one another in ministry throughout the world. Ignatius would not have written to Christians in any other place if he had not felt connected with them or supported by them. This theme of unity is all-pervasive within his letters, and one of his overarching concerns is that the unity they had be preserved.

Whereas the Didache saw the merging together (or replacing) of prophets and teachers with bishops and deacons, Ignatius knew a definitive threefold order of leaders within the church—bishops, presbyters, and deacons. These roles were not seen as hierarchical stepping-stones leading up the chain of command, but rather as three unique roles within the life of the church. Bishops were equated with shepherds, and also as God the Father for the life of the church. Presbyters were equated with the apostles and also the Sanhedrin, and the title is always plural. This means that an individual congregation, in Ignatius's understanding and experience, would have one bishop and several presbyters. Deacons were equated to Jesus Christ himself, since he came to serve and that was the deacons' role. Deacons were also uniquely called "ministers of the mysteries of Jesus Christ."[1] This is interesting because the original term for a *sacrament is mystery*. The Greek *mysterion* was translated into the Latin *sacramentum*. There is another, explicit statement concerning the sacraments from Ignatius as well. He wrote, "Let that be deemed a proper Eucharist which is administered either by the bishop, or by one to whom he has entrusted it." Ignatius also stated, "It is not lawful without the bishop either to baptize or to celebrate a love-feast."[2] For him, the role of the bishop was indispensable in the life of a congregation.

Despite these statements, one implicit and the other explicit, about who was involved with the celebration of the Lord's Supper, Ignatius also made an interesting statement. He said that the entire gathered body of believers were "within the altar" together.[3] This is the same terminology that was used in officiating at the Lord's Supper in later years, as the entire area of the church building in which the clergy stood during the service came to be called "the altar." Here in Ignatius, the idea of being within the altar is equated with the idea of being assembled together as the church. In other words, Ignatius understood that even though one person may stand before the entire assembly, the whole congregation is a collective participant in the sacramental life of the church. There is still the sense that it is the entire congregation that is the priesthood, and that one leader, the bishop (or potentially a deacon appointed by the bishop), stands at the forefront of the community as a representative of that gathering before God. This is why the emphasis on unity in the church was all-pervasive in Ignatius's

---

1 Ignatius, *The Epistle of Ignatius to the Trallians*, in *Ante-Nicene Fathers* (hereafter ANF), vol. 1, *Apostolic Fathers with Justin Martyr and Irenaeus*, ed. Alexander Roberts and James Donaldson (n.p.: Hendrickson, 1995), 67.2.
2 Ignatius, *The Epistle of Ignatius to the Smyrnaeans*, in ANF, 1.90.8.
3 Ignatius, *The Epistle of Ignatius to the Ephesians* in ANF, 1.51.5.

letters. This was how Ignatius understood worship as it was done sixty to seventy years after the founding of the church.

Chronologically, the next account of Christian worship did not even come from Christians. Less than a decade after Ignatius was martyred in Rome, Pliny the Younger was the governor of the Roman province of Bithynia-Pontus, the northern coast of modern Turkey. While he was administering this province, he regularly wrote to Trajan, the current emperor, to keep him informed about his province and to ask advice on certain issues. Around AD 112 Pliny wrote to the emperor regarding the "Christian problem." Christians were being denounced and imprisoned. Pliny had the obstinate ones executed after they confessed their faith three times. He released others who would offer a sacrifice to the Roman gods or curse Christ. Nevertheless, over time he began to feel uneasy about his course of action and sought out more information about this new religion. Perhaps the kinds of people being executed were not the normal sort of criminals, or perhaps the numbers of executions were excessive. Whatever the cause, Pliny wanted imperial backing for his course of action.

Under examination, Pliny found out that Christians met together before dawn on a specific day. He did not relate what day of the week this was, but based on the other accounts just mentioned, it most likely was the first day of the week. While the Christians were together, they "recite[d] by turns a form of words to Christ as a god" and then met later in the day for a meal together.[4] Because this in and of itself did not seem to merit the ire the empire had toward Christians, Pliny tortured two female slaves for more information. These two slaves were specifically identified as *deaconesses*.

From Pliny, then, it is noted that Christians had another group of people beyond those with differing spiritual gifts—bishops, presbyters/elders, and deacons. There were female deacons that were a distinct

---

[4] *A New Eusebius: Documents illustrating the history of the Church to AD 337*, 2nd revised edition, ed. J. Stephenson, (SPCK, 1987), 19.

position within the church. As well, worship was on a fixed day, before dawn, and there was some sort of unison or responsive reading within worship. This means that the entire community was involved in worship in some fashion. Implied in his letter could be that the Lord's Supper was regularly celebrated, as the nature of the meal was a cause of concern for Pliny as well as the fact that the Christians bound themselves with an oath—the literal understanding of the Latin *sacramentum*. He specifically noted that the meal the community shared was normal food. This could be a way to show he had investigated the charge of cannibalism against Christians, as the language of eating a body and drinking blood was regularly understood in that manner in the empire in these early days of the church.

Fewer than forty years after this letter, the most complete record of Christian worship was made. A Christian named Justin, now known as Justin Martyr, wrote a defense of Christianity to the Roman emperor Antonius Pius. This defense, his *First Apology*, explained the origins of the Christian faith, its major tenets of belief, and (most important for this book) a detailed account of worship. Up to this point in history, Christians kept what they did in worship out of any specific writings, not necessarily because they wanted to keep it secret, but because the majority of their writings were by Christians and for other Christians. They would already know what constituted Christian worship, because they were all involved in it and already participated in it. It was a natural and regular part of their lives, and the fact that anything was written concerning it before now is serendipitous. This writing, however, was by an informed Christian trying to explain to the emperor what Christians believed and did together. As a result, the account is very detailed. Once Justin arrived at the place in his apology where he talked about Christian worship and ritual, he first explained baptism, then the Eucharist, and finally gave a detailed account of a typical worship service. Because this account is of such value, it will not only be analyzed here, looking at who was involved in worship, but also in chapter 4, "The Order of Worship," and chapter 8, "The Sacrament of Holy Communion."

In his section on baptism, Justin did not specify who was involved in the rite. He made use of the pronoun *we* when referring to those participating:

> As many as are persuaded and believe that what we teach and say is true, and undertake to be able to live accordingly, are instructed to pray and entreat God with fasting, for the remission of their sins that are past, we pray and fast with them. Then they are brought by us where there is water, and are regenerated in the same manner in which we were ourselves regenerated.[5]

This may indicate that baptism was the responsibility of the entire community, or Justin may not have given all the exact information pertaining to the ritual. Whoever was involved in the actual ritual, one thing is certain: it was communal. While it may have been that the entire congregation was present, there was at least a representation of it, so that the newly baptized person understood that he or she was now a part of the community of believers. Justin made it clear in his section on the Eucharist that the baptism did not involve the entire congregation, nor was it at the church service proper. He opened this next section with the words

> But we, after we have thus washed him who has been convinced and has assented to our teaching, bring him to the place where those who are called brethren are assembled, in order that we may offer hearty prayers in common.[6]

Once the entire community was together, both the faithful and those newly baptized Christians, along with the ones (whoever they were) who were present and participated in baptizing them, the church

---

5 Justin Martyr, *The First Apology of Justin Martyr for the Christians Addressed to the Roman Senate*, in *ANF*, 1.183.61.

6 Justin Martyr, *The First Apology*, in *ANF*, 1.185.65.

celebrated the Lord's Supper. Justin gave a detailed account of who was involved in the rite:

> Having ended the prayers, we salute one another with a kiss. There is then brought to the president of the brethren bread and a cup of wine mixed with water; and he, taking them, gives praise and glory to the Father of the universe, through the name of the Son and of the Holy Ghost, and offers thanks at considerable length for our being counted worthy to receive these things at his hands. And when he has concluded the prayers and thanksgivings, all the people present express their assent by saying *Amen*. This word Amen answers in the Hebrew language to *so be it*. And when the president has given thanks, and all the people have expressed their assent, those who are called by us deacons give to each of those present to partake of the bread and wine mixed with water over which the thanksgiving was pronounced, and to those who are absent they carry away a portion.[7]

In this account Justin listed the president or leader of the brethren, the people, and the deacons. It was the role of the leader, and this may be a bishop or a presbyter, as he did not give any other detail as to who this may be, to preside over the ritual and pray a lengthy prayer over the bread and cup. This, as will be discussed more fully in chapter 8, was absolutely necessary for worship in Justin's experience. Equally essential, however, was that all of the people together must assent to what was happening on behalf of them. Without their Amen, the service was not complete. Only then, after the leader's prayer and the entire congregation's assent, did the deacons administer the sacrament to the people and take it to those who were not in attendance with the rest of the congregation. This is a wonderful image of how, even at this early stage of history within the church (approximately 120 years after the crucifixion), and even with significant development of congregational life together in worship, the presider was still seen as one

---

7   Justin Martyr, *First Apology*, in *ANF*, 1.185.65.

acting on behalf of the entire community. The whole community together was required to be able to celebrate the sacrament. This is an example of the priesthood of all gathered, as they all must assent to what was said and done on their behalf by the leader.

Justin specifically named one more person as having a part within the worship of the community. In his section on the actual worship service, Justin gave a basic order for worship. Within that order, he made mention of a designated *reader*, who would read from the Gospels and/or the Old Testament "as long as time permits." This was mostly due to the reality that individual Bibles were not yet in existence and many could not read. If the Christians were going to understand Scripture, it would have to be by hearing it read in the context of a worship service. The only writings a community would have would be the property of the entire congregation and only brought out during a service. Therefore, many of the readings were quite long, so that the congregation could be exposed to as much scripture as possible. After the reader was finished, the president expounded the readings in a sermon. After the sermon, the entire congregation prayed together. Then the celebration of the Eucharist began. It is not stated with certainty whether or not the reader was a specific role or just someone who was asked to read.

Who's Who in Worship

That people are necessary for worship is a given, especially since *liturgy* literally means "the work of the people." The question, though, is which people. From the earliest days of the church, according to the New Testament writings, there were people with certain spiritual gifts given by God to conduct ministry and participate in worship. Over time, as seen earlier, these gifted people were either given titles or were replaced by other roles. Despite there being certain distinct and definitive roles within the church, according to Justin Martyr, worship was still seen as a communal event in which all the people participated as late as AD 150. Yet over time there was increasing specialization within worship of a few key roles and individuals. The church may have begun with worship being a communal event where everyone participated to a greater or lesser extent, but the fact that one of the key platforms of the Protestant Reformation was the idea of recapturing the priesthood of all believers shows that this idea was lost over time.

Without getting bogged down in the historical development of every role within the church, here is a list of what became the defined roles within worship in the Western and Eastern churches within another two hundred years of Justin:

WESTERN CHURCH	EASTERN CHURCH
bishop	bishop
priest (presbyter/elder)	priest (presbyter/elder)
deacon	deacon
acolyte	subdeacon
reader (lector)	reader
	chanter

The titles of each role convey specific duties to be performed during worship services. The roles of bishop, priest, and deacon are considered the major orders of the church, and the other orders are considered *minor* orders. The difference between the two classes of orders was ordination. For the major orders, the recipient was ordained. For the minor orders, the recipient was not ordained. In the Western church there were also the minor orders of porter, or doorkeeper, and exorcist, as well as the lowest-level major order of subdeacon, until 1972.

While this scheme may seem overly complicated, it is important to remember that as the church grew and developed, so did the system by which people served in worship. As well, while each of the levels of service with its corresponding title could be a permanent place of service, usually this was the ascending order in preparation for ministry. Within the Protestant movement, the Methodists, quite unintentionally, came close to this scheme when it first became an independent church in the late 1700s. The various roles or orders of ministry within the Methodist Episcopal Church were as follows:

METHODIST EPISCOPAL CHURCH
bishop (superintendent)
traveling elder
traveling deacon
traveling preacher
local preacher
exhorter
class leader

In this scheme, the major orders would be bishop, elder, and deacon; the minor orders were the rest.[8]

As the life of the church continued through the centuries, and as more and more orders and specific roles were created or identified within the worshiping community, an unfortunate side effect occurred. The congregation as a whole became disengaged from worship. An attitude of clericalism—that only those with official roles (often ordained) could or should do anything with respect to worship—encroached upon the people. This attitude took many forms and was experienced in various ways over the years. Latin, once the universal language of western Europe, but now known only to the clergy and the educated, was the language of worship. Corporate prayers vanished, participation in the Eucharist was virtually nonexistent, and even the congregation's *Amen* was no longer necessary due to the development of the *missa privata*, the private Mass, where only the priest and perhaps one server were present. By the time of the Reformation in the sixteenth and seventeenth centuries, the average parishioner

---

8   One of the interesting aspects of Methodist polity is that the offices of bishop and elder are the same, bishop being a specific role within the order of elder. Nevertheless, Methodists still consecrate and set apart their bishops, and even Wesley wrote of ordaining Thomas Coke as a bishop originally.

was little more than a spectator at a worship service, if he or she even attended it. Christian worship ceased being the *work of the people* and became the *work of the professionals*. It was against this concept of the work of the professionals that the theology of the priesthood of all believers was recaptured in the Protestant Reformation. The reformers tried to make the mark of baptism as the relevant sacrament for ministry rather than ordination and to turn the tide of participation in worship from clergy to the whole congregation. More of this will be discussed in the next chapter.

Despite the Protestant rediscovery and implementation of the priesthood of all believers, in congregations today there is still a danger of this kind of clericalism. The worship service could still be constructed and executed in such a way that the people feel as if they are little more than spectators. A congregation's leadership may still give the impression that worship is the work of talented, trained professionals rather than of the whole people of God. These professionals may be musicians or those who interpret the Bible. And they may truly be professionals (being paid for their services), or it may just be the congregation's perception based up the attitudes reinforced by a particular congregation. Because of this potential misunderstanding in worship, it is necessary to have, not only a solid historical understanding of the development of worship, but also a solid theological understanding of ordination and how God calls the church to worship. That is the subject of the next chapter.

THE THEOLOGY OF ORDINATION

In the earliest days of the church, it seems there was a gifts-based understanding of leadership. This can be seen in several places, most notably Ephesians 4:22-23. There Paul wrote about how the Holy Spirit had gifted certain people for the work of ministry. Over the years, as congregations became more established and they had second- or third-generation members, the giftedness qualification became subsumed within a role-based understanding of leadership. This is seen in the Didache and other texts referenced in the previous chapter, where the specific positions of bishop, presbyter/elder, and deacon/deaconess took precedence. This does not mean that those who were in these roles were not gifted for ministry. Rather, it means that leadership within the church was identified not so much by specific gifting but by specific roles. To make a shift such as this, though, there must be a theological reason for those roles, usually the ordained roles. In other words, there must be a theology of ordination: who is ordained, why, and for what purpose.

Today there are two main understandings of ordination. Both of these views have the same starting point, yet, subsequently, they move in different directions. Beginning with the idea that the whole community of the church is a priesthood and that different members of that community have different roles, ordination then becomes part of only a few of those roles. Here is where the difference now arises. One understanding of ordination is that the one ordained is empowered by the Holy Spirit "to act in the person of Christ the head, for the service of all the members of the church. The ordained minister is, as it were, an 'icon' of Christ the priest."[1] Another understanding of ordination is that the one ordained is empowered by the Holy Spirit to be "a primary representation of God's love."[2] While this difference may seem subtle, it is the key distinction between viewing ordination as a sacrament that communicates a new and different grace to a baptized Christian and a rite that acknowledges a role that is set apart within the larger body of baptized Christians. These distinctions will be discussed further momentarily, but before that analysis can happen, it is essential to gain a historical understanding of ordination within the church.

The Early Church

Scripture lists the roles of both the bishop/presbyter and the deacon/deaconess. Romans 16 lists Phoebe as a deacon and Junia as an apostle.[3] Philippians is addressed to "bishops and deacons" (1:1). First Timothy 3 gives qualifications for bishops and deacons. Titus discusses presbyters/elders and bishops. First Peter 5 gives admonitions to elders. The books of 2 and 3 John were written by "The elder." Finally, in Acts 20 Paul calls together the elders of the Ephesian church and addresses them as *episcopous*, literally, bishops. Along with these references are also the lists of spiritual gifts in 1 Corinthians 12–14 and Ephesians 4:11-16. Even with all of these different leadership positions, there is precious little about who actually did what within the context of a worship service. This is because no one needed to write about what everyone in the community already knew about worship. It was being practiced, so there was no need to go into detail.

To begin to see these activities explained, it is necessary to read those writings from the next generation of the church. A few of these

---

1 *Catechism of the Catholic Church*, ¶1142.
2 *The Book of Discipline of The United Methodist Church, 2016* (Nashville: The United Methodist Publishing House, 2016), ¶303.2.
3 The title of apostle quickly fell to the wayside after the first century. In early-second-century writings, the apostles are equated with the priests or bishops in duties, responsibilities, and authority.

writings have already been discussed in chapter 1, namely, the Didache and the writings of Ignatius of Antioch. The theology of ordination that is described within the Didache shows a transition from the gifts-based roles of prophet and teacher to the role-based leadership of bishop and deacon. All four of these positions, teacher and prophet, bishop and deacon, are seen in continuity with the role of the high priest at the temple in Jerusalem. There are definitive people for definitive duties within the worshiping community, and those people are seen in a sacramental, or sacerdotal, function. It is their duty to oversee the sacrifice for the community.

In between the Didache and Ignatius is Clement's *Epistle to the Corinthians*, which he wrote in the 90s to the church in Corinth. The church was once again divided. This time it was because some of the members either tried to overthrow their bishop in favor of someone else, or succeeded. Clement wrote that the apostles "appointed the first-fruits . . . to be bishops and deacons of those who should afterwards believe."[4] In chapter 44 he continued:

> Our apostles also knew, through our Lord Jesus Christ, and there would be strife on account of the office of the episcopate. For this reason, therefore, inasmuch as they had obtained a perfect fore-knowledge of this, they appointed those [ministers] already mentioned, and afterwards gave instructions, that when these would fall asleep, other approved men should succeed them in their ministry. We are of opinion therefore, that those appointed by them, or afterwards by other eminent men, with the consent of the whole church, and who have blamelessly served the flock of Christ in a humble, peaceable, and disinterested spirit, and have for a long time possessed the good opinion of all, cannot be justly dismissed from the ministry. For our sin will not be small, if we eject from the episcopate those who have blamelessly and holily fulfilled its duties. Blessed are those presbyters who, having finished their course before now, have

---

4 Clement, *The First Epistle of Clement to the Corinthians*, in *ANF*, 1.16.42.

obtained a fruitful and perfect departure [from this world]; for they have no fear lest any one deprive them of the place now appointed them.[5]

In this letter Clement mentioned bishops, presbyters, and deacons. In addition, it seems that the role of bishop and presbyter were interchangeable for him, as they were for many of the early writings of the church.

In Ignatius of Antioch's writings, there was a threefold scheme of bishop-presbyter/elder-deacon that led the church. Unlike Clement's, Ignatius's writings presupposed one bishop, a group of elders, and another group of deacons all in ministry together, and all with distinct roles. In one letter Ignatius directly stated:

> Let that be deemed a proper Eucharist which is [administered] either by the bishop or by one to whom he has entrusted it . . . It is not lawful without the bishop either to baptize or to celebrate a love-feast; but whatsoever he shall approve of, that is also pleasing to God, so that everything that is done may be secure and valid.[6]

The next major treatment of clergy in the early church was from Irenaeus of Lyon. Although Irenaeus was bishop in Lyon (known as Lyon in modern-day France and as Lugdunum in Gaul during Roman times), he was from Asia Minor. Historical evidence points to him being a disciple of Polycarp, who was in turn a disciple of John the apostle. The majority of the work that survives from Irenaeus's writings is his *Against Heresies*, in which he systematically categorized various Gnostic heresies, known to him either through reading their works or interacting with them personally and his refutations of them.

Throughout this work, one of the major defenses Irenaeus used to combat the new, novel, and false teachings of the Gnostics was

---

5   Clement, in *ANF*, 1.17.44.
6   Ignatius, *The Epistle of Ignatius to the Smyrnaeans*, in *ANF*, 1.89.8.

what he termed apostolic succession. He wrote, "The blessed apostles, then, having founded and built up the church, committed into the hands of Linus the office of the episcopate [of Rome]."[7] After continuing the list of succeeding bishops from the time of Linus to his own, Irenaeus further wrote:

> In this order, and by this succession, the ecclesiastical tradition from the apostles, and the preaching of the truth, have come down to us. And this is most abundant proof that there is one and the same vivifying faith, which has been preserved in the church from the apostles until now, and handed down in truth.[8]

Unlike Ignatius, whose main concern was for order and unity within worship and most typified in the celebration of one Eucharist by the bishop (or one appointed by the bishop), Irenaeus's concern was for unity in teaching the faith. This unity was also found in the office of the bishop, whose teaching was seen in a direct line back to the original apostles.

With the Didache, Clement, Ignatius, and Irenaeus, a picture emerges of what the duties and roles of the ordained clergy meant by the early third century. In this composite picture, the role of the bishop, or sometimes the bishop/presbyter since the separation of these two offices was not yet complete in all places, is one that gradually took over the role of prophet or teacher in the church, being seen as the Christian version of the high priest in the temple. It was the bishop's responsibility to ensure that the church celebrated the Eucharist together, and that the apostles' teaching was the teaching that was still being offered to the church. These bishops were chosen by the apostles to be the leaders in the local churches, and when the time came for them to step aside, they chose new bishops to succeed them.

---

7   Irenaeus, *Against Heresies* 3.3.3, in *ANF*, 1.416.
8   Irenaeus, in *ANF*, 1.416.

The Roman Catholic Position

From these early statements regarding ordination, the office, duties, and understanding of those who are ordained expanded. Eventually, what is still the official Roman Catholic position was formulated by Thomas Aquinas in *Summa Theologica*. He wrote:

> Now Christ is the fountain-head of the entire priesthood: for the priest of the Old Law was a figure of Him; while the priest of the New Law works in His person, according to 2 Corinthians 2:10, "For what I have pardoned, if I have pardoned anything, for your sakes have I done it in the person of Christ."[9]

This is the theological understanding of ordination as a sacrament, and that the recipient of that sacrament now stands *in persona Christi*, in the person of Christ. The main issue with this understanding of ordination is that ministry is ultimately Christ's and Christ's alone. Humans only participate in Christ's ministry by receiving from him a special grace to be more completely enveloped by him. All Christians, by virtue of their baptism, are incorporated into Christ, but not all Christians have this further and deeper experience of grace. To be completely forthright in this understanding of ordination, it is also necessary to state that it is actually the ordination of the bishop that is most fully identified as being in persona Christi. As such, the bishop is the only one who actually has the authority and grace to ordain others. By this act, the bishop conveys grace to a priest to share in that position just as Christ shared this grace and position with the bishop.

Because ordination mediates further grace to the Christian, it is by definition a sacrament. Within Roman Catholic theology some of the sacraments are repeatable, such as Eucharist and penance (confession), and some of them are not repeatable, such as baptism and confirmation. Ordination is in the non-repeatable category. Practically,

---

9 Thomas Aquinas, *Summa Theologica*, 3.22.4.3.

then, ordination is seen as making an indelible mark on one's soul, just like baptism. Through the grace conveyed in the sacrament of ordination, the priest is ontologically changed, changed in his being, similar to the change in being when one is baptized. The priest is now incorporated into Christ not just through baptism as a part of the body of Christ, but into Christ's authority and headship over the church. In this way, Jesus Christ himself is still the priest of the church and still exercises all priestly functions for the church, but he does so through the ordained priest. This takes seriously the high priesthood of Christ in the Book of Hebrews as well as the passage from 2 Corinthians Aquinas quoted earlier.

If the priest stands *in persona Christi*, then the priest must reflect Christ as perfectly as possible. This is the reason for continued adherence to two rules for ordination that have caused considerable discussion, both in ecumenical dialogue and within the Roman Catholic Church in recent years: an all-male priesthood and clerical celibacy. Since the priest is in the place of Christ, the priest ought to look like Christ in every way possible. Christ was male; therefore, priests must be male. Christ was not married; therefore, priests must be celibate. There is much historical, biblical, and theological precedent for a married priesthood. In fact, the universal requirement for a celibate priesthood in the Roman church did not arise until the Middle Ages, and then it was primarily a response to the church's increasing wealth and the desire to root out corrupt priests and bishops who acted as feudal lords, passing down the church's wealth and property to their children. Before this, there was no directive that priests had to be unmarried. It was recommended, but not required. If the Roman Catholic Church would ever modify their requirements for ordination, mandatory celibacy would be the most likely option to be changed. The adherence to an all-male priesthood, however, is extremely unlikely due to this theology of being *in persona Christi*.

The Protestant Position

One of the rallying cries of the Protestant Reformation was the priesthood of all believers. It was a reaction against the clericalism in the church of the day and a way to remind its adherents that all Christians are on equal footing before God. All Christians are baptized into Christ; therefore, all Christians share in the ministry of Christ. There is no separate class of Christian within the church who receive more of Christ's grace than everyone else. All are a part of the one body, and all have the one and same Spirit at work within them for the particular ministry to which God calls them.

In this framework, ordination was no longer considered a sacrament. While it may conform to the classic definition of a sacrament, having an outward sign (laying on of hands) that signifies an inward grace (ordination), because it was not for all people, it could not be a sacrament. Just as marriage was not for all people, ordination was not for all people. Therefore, it ought not to be considered a sacrament if it was only for a select group within the church. Various Protestant groups (and eventually denominations) provided for the leadership of their movements using different means in the absence of a sacramental ordination. Some continued with ordination rites that were divested of sacramental theology. Some moved to congregational acclamation and prayer for leaders. Some simply acknowledged the perceived gifts for leadership among their members without any formal ceremony. Practically, some groups apparently retained a threefold understanding of ordained ministry with bishops, presbyter/elders, and deacons. Some eliminated the office of bishop but retained elders and deacons. Some redefined elders and deacons but retained ordination. And some had no ordination at all.

Whatever the format of ordination within Protestant communities, the net result was the same. The focus was no longer on the ordained person standing in persona Christi, but rather Protestant churches acknowledged a specific ministry within the body of Christ under the authority of the priesthood granted to all Christians by virtue of baptism. The main way of viewing the ceremony (if there was one) was no longer ontological but rather functional. All Christians already had an ontological change into the likeness of Christ at conversion; therefore, all Christians stand *in persona Christi* as they are faithful to their baptismal vows. In essence, it was a return to a gifts-based ministry concept, all the while retaining a mode of setting one apart that looked (in some cases) like the sacramental ordination the church had come to know and practice.

The Methodist Position

Methodism is an interesting case, because it was born out of the Church of England, in which there is a much more convoluted understanding of ordination. When the Church of England formed, the directive was that nothing should change except the ultimate source of authority. No longer would the pope in Rome be the visible head of the church. Now that position would be filled by the reigning British monarch. Thus, Henry VIII became the head of the Church of England. Despite this change, since a significant portion of the church did not wish to separate from Rome, the Church of England retained much of the pre-Reformation theology. As such, there was a high degree of understanding in the Anglican tradition for ordination being sacramental.

Along with the Roman Catholic theological tradition, there was also Reformed theology at play within Anglicanism. It was this theological strand within the church that helped it definitively decide that there were only two sacraments, baptism and the Lord's Supper. Since ordination was no longer a sacrament, the official theology of the rite was to confirm and set apart leaders within the church for specific ministries. However, the ordination rite still contained language that asked for the Holy Spirit to be given to the ordinands to empower them to fulfill the office to which they were ordained, not as a subset of the ministry to which all Christians were called, but as a special and distinct ministry. This ordination could only be conferred by a bishop, and only one rightly ordained could administer the sacraments. While the specific statement of *in persona Christi* was not a part of the understanding of ordination, nevertheless there was language in the Thirty-nine Articles of Religion that could have been interpreted in that manner. One of the articles (art. 26) was on the sacraments being celebrated by ministers who were not living holy lives. It contained the statement:

> Although in the visible church the evil be ever mingled with the good, and sometimes the evil has chief authority in the Ministration of the Word and Sacraments, yet forasmuch as they do not the same in their own name, but in Christ's, and do minister by his commission and authority, we may use their Ministry, both in hearing the Word of God, and in receiving of the Sacraments.[10]

While this does not use the specific language of "in the person of Christ," it has the exact same meaning. The ordained minister performs the sacramental duties of the office in Christ's name and by Christ's authority.

John Wesley was very much a product of this confusing ecclesial understanding of ordination. It was not a sacrament but was treated as such. It was a consecration to a specialized ministry within the entire priesthood of all believers, yet it used language very reminiscent of the theology of *in persona Christi*. As an ordained priest in the Church of England, Wesley affirmed this situation. He lived in the ambiguity of the nature of Anglican ordination, as he affirmed the general call to ministry of all believers in Christ and understood that the sacramental ministry was restricted to only those who had been properly ordained according to the church's polity, rites, and tradition. Within the movement he helped found, Wesley carried this muddled distinction with him and made it a hallmark of the Methodist movement. Wesley made

---

10 *Book of Common Prayer.*

a significant distinction between those who had a calling to preach and those who were ordained to administer the sacraments. By making this distinction, Wesley was able to justify setting up meeting houses and new fellowships within parish boundaries all over England and Ireland precisely because none of his preachers were ordained. They were not in schism from the church because they were not administering the sacraments to the Methodists gathered in these meetings.

When it became necessary for one section of Methodism to have its own ordained clergy, due to the American Revolution and the flight of Anglican clergy from the former American colonies, Wesley muddled the Anglican situation even more: he formed a presbytery and ordained clergy himself. But why would it be *necessary* for Methodism to have access to an ordained clergy? It is precisely because Wesley understood ordination in the Anglican sense of still having a sacramental aspect to it that made it necessary. Only those who were properly ordained had the authority to administer the sacraments. Without access to ordained clergy, the American Methodists would not have access to baptism or the Lord's Supper. As these were powerful means of grace within Wesley's theology, the Lord's Supper being the means of grace par excellence, it was unfathomable for Christians to be without access to them. Therefore, in September 1784, after Wesley had tried and failed to have the bishop of London ordain even one Methodist preacher to go to America, Wesley took the questionable step of performing the ordinations himself. It was questionable because this could be interpreted as separating from the Church of England, a charge that some made against Wesley, but his theology and his understanding of ordination led him to conclude this was the only way to solve the existing problem. Therefore, he and several ordained priests laid their hands on Thomas Coke and ordained him a superintendent (bishop), as well as ordaining Thomas Vasey and Richard Whatcoat as elders for what would become the Methodist Episcopal Church in America. So controversial was this decision that John hid it even from his brother Charles, who was much more conservative in his approach to solving problems. Charles, who was not pleased with the whole event, wrote a poem about it:

> So easily are Bishops made
> > By man's or woman's whim?
> W[esley] his hands on C[oke] hath laid,
> > But who laid hands on Him?
>
> Hands on himself he laid, and *took*
> > An Apostolic Chair;
> And then ordain'd his Creature C[oke]
> > His Heir and Successor.
>
> Episcopalians, now no more
> > With Presbyterians fight,
> But give your needless Contest o're,
> > 'Whose Ordination's right?'
>
> It matter not, if Both are One,
> > Or different in degree,
> For lo! ye see contain'd in ~~Prelate~~ [*sic*] John
> > The whole Presbytery![11]

It is absolutely no wonder contemporary Methodism has such a hard time arriving at a workable theology of ordination. Almost every single possible interpretation of ordination and ministry is present within it. From Anglicanism there is a Roman Catholic sacramental strand and a Protestant strand from Continental reformation influence. From the beginning of the Methodist movement there was a gifts-based strand with the itinerant preachers who were distinct from the ordained clergy in the Church of England. From Wesley's own ordinations there was a Presbyterian/Congregational strand. Almost all theological traditions pertaining to ordination are present in Methodism. These are just from

---

11 Frank Baker, ed., *Representative Verse of Charles Wesley* (Nashville: Epworth Press and Abingdon Press, 1962), 368.

the initial founding of Methodism as a movement and as an independent church. This analysis does nothing for the next two hundred years' doctrinal development and practice within the various bodies that are descendent from Wesley's original movement.

Nevertheless, there is still a discernable theology of ordination within Methodism that makes sense of all these different theological strands. The key to understanding a Methodist theology of ordination is in looking at why there is ordination in the first place. For the Roman Catholic tradition, it is so the priest can stand in the place of Christ and be an icon of Christ. For Methodism, it is so the ordained minister can be "a primary representation of God's love."[12] Notice the shift in emphasis. The Roman Catholic understanding is Christocentric, rooted in the person of Jesus Christ. It is Christ's ministry and authority that are passed on to the ordained person. In the Methodist understanding, the entire Trinity is represented because the ordained person becomes an icon, not of Christ, but of God's love.

The love of God is best illustrated with the theological term *perichoresis*, the mutual indwelling of each of the persons of the Trinity one with another. It is not the high priesthood of Jesus Christ that is represented in ministry. It is the self-sacrificial love and service of the Trinity that is represented in ministry. This is the same type of life and service to which all Christians are called by virtue of baptism and being members of the priesthood of all believers, but it is set apart in a visible and iconic form in the one who is ordained. Just as Jesus Christ made the invisible God visible for all of creation to see, so too ordination makes the invisible commitment to a Christian lifestyle of love and service visible in the life of the minister. In this understanding, it is perfectly natural that the tasks specifically relegated to ordained ministry are the sacraments of the Lord's Supper and baptism. In these two acts by the church, the love of God is clearly made manifest. Both of

---

12 *Book of Discipline of The United Methodist Church, 2016*, ¶303.2.

these sacraments show the love of Christ in that they both re-present the death and resurrection of Jesus for the sake of the church and the world. If the ordained minister is an icon of the love of God, then it is only logical that the signs and actions that best communicate that love to the world be administered by that minister.

Women in Ministry

One more important aspect of ordination must be mentioned in relation to this theology. Both male and female can be ordained. Since the ordained minister is an icon of the love of God, and not specifically of the human person of Jesus Christ, the one being ordained does not have to bear the responsibility of being like Jesus in gender. Since the Holy Spirit gifts all Christians for ministry, and since in Christ there is neither male nor female, those being ordained for ministry to demonstrate and share the love of God in the world at large can be either male or female. There is no restriction on this aspect of ministry. This theology, then, actually takes a more biblical approach to ministry than the Roman Catholic tradition of an all-male priesthood. By having ordained ministers represent the totality of the Trinity in the Godhead's love for humanity, it validates women in leadership positions within the covenant people of God from the Old Testament to the present. This would include women such as Deborah and Huldah as well as Phoebe, Junia, Priscilla, and the women who prophesied in the Corinthian church.

Many pages have been written both supporting and attacking the ordination of women. Much of the language is hurtful to our sisters in Christ, whether they feel called to ordained ministry or not. The reality is that ordination as is known and practiced in the church today does not have a biblical mandate. There are, as seen earlier, gifts-based ministries within the pages of the New Testament. There are women who obviously held various roles within the church throughout the New Testament, as evidenced by the women who prophesy in various places.

Prophecy in the New Testament is most directly correlated to preaching today in congregations around the world. They were women preachers. The only injunctions against women teaching within the church are found in letters that were written to specific congregations dealing with particular issues in those congregations. Much current scholarship has investigated those passages and put them in their appropriate context.[13]

There is also a clear trajectory within the Bible to deal with the role of women as part of the covenant people of God. The first place to look is the origin of the two biological sexes in Genesis. The creation account has two important points to make with respect to human beings. First, both male and female were made in the image and likeness of God. One was not subordinated to the other. Second, the only portion of creation that was not good was the man without woman. Everything else that was created was immediately declared good by God. The first time something was not good was when the man was alone. Woman was created to be an *ezer*, usually translated as *helper* or *helpmate*. This does not mean that the woman was created to simply assist the man, as the very same word was used of God in helping Israel numerous times in the Old Testament. In fact, the name *Eliezer* literally means "God is my helper." Women were not subordinated to men until the Fall, as a part of the curse. This fact, in and of itself, should be enough to show that women and men ought to have full and equal participation within the church.

Paul stated in Galatians 3:28, "There is no longer Jew or Greek, there is no longer slave or free, there is no longer male and female; for all of you are one in Christ Jesus." This passage has been interpreted by those who do not wish to extend ordination rights to women as making both male and female equal in salvation but still separate in

---

[13] For an excellent treatment of 1 Timothy, see Gary G. Hoag's work, *Wealth in Ancient Ephesus and the First Letter to Timothy: Fresh Insights from* Ephesica *by Xenophon of Ephesus* (Winona Lake, IN: Eisenbrauns, 2015).

roles within the church. The problem with that interpretation is that no one would say the same about the Jew/Gentile divide or the slave/free divide. There is also another interpretation of this passage that claims that Paul was merely subverting a common Jewish prayer in which a Jewish male thanked God that he was not born a Gentile, a slave, or a woman. The problem with that interpretation is that this prayer is only found in the Talmud around AD 200, well after Paul wrote this letter. More likely, Paul was making a significant statement with this one verse that in Christ all of the divisions in the world are undone. This is because these divisions were the first three significant divisions recorded in Genesis, in reverse order. Abraham was called out to create a covenant people in Genesis 12; Noah cursed Canaan to be a slave in Genesis 9; and females were subordinated to males, creating a hierarchy within humanity, in Genesis 3. In Christ even the most ancient divisions are restored. Seen in this light, it is no wonder that Paul would work side by side in ministry with Titus, a Greek who was left in charge of ordering the ministry and congregations in Crete; Onesimus, a slave who was restored to his master, Philemon, and later became the bishop of Ephesus; and Phoebe, the female deacon in Romans 16 who was called a *prostasis*, literally one who *stands in front of* the congregation in Cenchreae. This term is also related to modern the Greek title *proistamenos*, one who *presides or leads*. The most common English term that would be equal to it would be *rector*. Unfortunately, many English translations render the word as *benefactor*, which belies the leadership role the title conveys.

Despite some interpretation of the concept of *in persona Christi*, there is no reason why women should not be included in those who can be ordained to become an icon of the love of the Trinity for the world. Biblically, the evidence is clear that God raised up female leaders in both the Old and New Testaments. Some, like Phoebe, were leaders in local congregations. Some were apostles, like Priscilla and Junia. Some were prophets in the modern sense of preachers. Some, like Huldah in 2 Kings 22:13-20 and 2 Chronicles 34:22-28, instructed both King Josiah and Hilkiah, the high priest, after the discovery of the Law in the temple. What is fascinating about this particular incident is not only was a woman the one instructing both the king and high priest, but this was four years after Jeremiah had begun his prophetic ministry. That is directly counter to the argument put forward by some in various branches of the church that God will condescend to use a woman in ministry if no man is available or willing to be in ministry. God has always included women in leadership, even teaching roles, and Christ destroyed the portion of the curse that led to the subjugation of women to men once and for all. The ordination of women should be a mark of the new creation in which all humanity is once again equal before God, called to service by God, and empowered by the Holy Spirit as God so chooses. Ironically, it is those Protestant denominations that seem the most anti–Roman Catholic in their polity and theology that use a Roman Catholic tradition and theology of ordination, rather than the plain reading of scripture, to justify their refusal of women's ordination.

Practical Issues

This theology of ordination, that of an icon of God's love, raises an interesting issue specifically for Methodism. Throughout the various branches and denominations of the Wesleyan/Methodist movement, we have people who are given the privilege of administering the sacraments who are not ordained. If the above theology of ordination is true, it would necessarily follow that only those who are ordained would be permitted to preside over baptism and the Lord's Supper. In fact, this was the driving force for ordinations in the beginning of the movement, John Wesley not wanting his Methodists in America to be without the sacraments. For decades afterward, Methodists still restricted administration of the sacraments only to ordained elders. Ordained deacons were not even permitted to administer the sacraments, and that was entirely within the historic tradition of the church, owing to Wesley's own experiences within the Church of England. Congregations that did not have an ordained person as the primary minister would not celebrate the sacraments until such a time as someone ordained was present. Often this was at a quarterly meeting, or it was when the itinerant preacher arrived at that particular congregation along the route. In the absence of the elder, local preachers would lead worship and conduct pastoral care, but it was the elder who baptized people and celebrated the Lord's Supper.

Yet currently in many of the Wesleyan/Methodist families, people who are not ordained are given the responsibility of administering the sacraments. They are called by various titles depending on the particular denomination, but the reality is the same across the spectrum. Whether they are local pastors, licensed preachers, conference ministerial candidates, or some other name, they are not ordained and can administer the sacraments within their local congregation. The United Methodist Church saw this incongruity—the fact that non-ordained individuals were able to administer the Lord's Supper and deacons (who are ordained) were not allowed to administer—so in 2012 deacons were given this authority and responsibility in the absence of an elder.

Practically speaking, for most Methodist denominations ordination no longer has as much to do with showing forth God's love in the administration of the sacraments. Too many other people are given the privilege of doing that very act, so the meaning behind it as a mark of ordination has become diluted to the point where it is now nonexistent. There is no difference sacramentally between an elder and a lay minister (of whatever title) as both can celebrate Holy Communion in their respective congregations. Currently there seems to be only two differences. First, an elder promises to itinerate. Ordination within Methodism has a traveling aspect to it, although not as much as it once had. Often, in the earliest days of Methodism, itinerant preachers would travel around circuits, and their assigned circuits would be changed every six months or every year. Eventually, most of Methodism settled on two to three years for an appointment, and the ordained minister would travel to the next appointment after that time was done. Today, with the conventional wisdom leaning toward longer appointments and increasingly complicated family dynamics of two-income households, itinerating essentially means that the ordained minister agrees, in principle, to go wherever sent. In practice, however, this simply means that an elder can administer the sacraments in venues beyond the local church to which the pastor is appointed, unlike a local pastor, whose sacramental authority is fixed to one particular congregation.

Second, clergy have their membership within the Annual Conference rather than a local congregation and are able to vote as clergy in conference matters. Non-ordained pastors may be given sacramental authority by the bishop, but they are still laypersons. As such, their membership is in a local congregation, and they are not allowed to vote as clergy on many of the issues that are discussed at Annual Conference. However, some lay ministers in this category are allowed to vote on certain clergy issues but not others. Often this restriction is placed upon voting on the ordination of others or voting on salary issues for clergy. Some in this category are "neither fish nor fowl" in that they are forbidden to vote on clergy issues because they are not ordained, yet they are forbidden to vote on lay issues because they are serving a congregation.

The irony of this peculiar take on ordination within Methodism is that it is very similar to the common notion of reducing baptism to membership within a congregation. Baptism, as will be discussed in chapter 7, has numerous levels of meaning and significance. Yet in many congregations it has been seen in a singular light of becoming a member of the congregation, and thus the denomination. Ordination, in a sense, has had the same reduction of meaning for many Methodists. Where once it was seen with a sacramental understanding, not necessarily a sacrament itself but rather necessary to administer the sacraments, now it is seen as simply membership within an annual conference.

3

SACRED SPACES

If this introduction is to use a common grammar to understand and interpret worship, it is necessary to not only see the "nouns" as the people involved in worship but also the places for worship. To be sure, since the whole of the universe is filled with the presence of God and the psalmists so rightly declared that there is no place where one could hide in creation from God, the issue of specific spaces for worship seems almost inconsequential. Yet specific places of worship, of encountering God, have been a part of the covenant people's story ever since God called Abram to leave one space and move to another.

Over the course of time, that general call turned into certain locations and hastily erected shrines. It took on new meaning when Moses brought down the Ten Commandments at a certain location, Sinai, and with the demarcation of holy and sacred space in the midst of the people, the tabernacle. The tabernacle gave way to the permanent fixture of the temple, and that in turn, was augmented by the establishment of the synagogue. Throughout all of this development, space that was set apart for special use by the people of God became integral for the purpose of worship and discipleship. These are some of the roots for the concept of sacred versus secular space.

This is the heritage that the Christian movement inherited and appropriated for its own. In the earliest days of the church, when the believers were mostly confined to Jerusalem, they met in each other's homes as well as in the temple. If Paul is any representative of how early missionaries acted, as the movement spread throughout the

Roman Empire, homes and local synagogues were used as bases of operation until the new group relocated to another location. Meeting in homes seemed to be the earliest spaces Christians used for worship, and then Christians began having dedicated spaces exclusively for worship; they built churches.

One of the earliest church buildings found is in the ruins of Dura-Europos, a city in modern Syria. This was an outpost near the Persian border, and sometime before AD 256 the building was intentionally buried as a way to reinforce the wall against the attacking Persians, since it was next to the wall. Many such buildings suffered the same fate, being seen as expendable in light of the oncoming forces. Because the town was abandoned after this war, the building was left for archaeologists to find. The building itself was a home that had been converted into a church. It had space for the congregation to gather, due to a wall being torn down between two rooms. It also had a separate baptistery that was large enough for people to stand while water was poured over their heads. The walls were covered in biblical imagery, retelling many of the most beloved stories. Interestingly, the style of paintings as well as the layout of the church closely resembled the synagogue in the same town, which was also buried in an effort to shore up defenses. This shows the Jewish roots of early Christianity and may indicate that the earliest generations of Christians intentionally continued Jewish modes of gathering and worship as they developed their own liturgical traditions. The synagogue was larger and more decorated, but the two buildings were similar enough for archaeologists to take notice.

Shortly after the Dura-Europos church was abandoned, there was a lull in the persecution of the church. During this time, leading up to the last major Roman persecution under Diocletian in AD 303, church buildings began to appear in many cities throughout the empire. These buildings were either renovated or intentionally built to be used exclusively for worship and catechetical instruction. The church buildings were so ubiquitous throughout the urban areas of the empire that when Diocletian initiated his persecution of the church, he could see a church building from his balcony in his capital of Nicomedia. Because of this he debated whether or not to burn it to the ground. He decided that it was too close to other buildings to risk a fire, so he had soldiers physically destroy the building. The fact that a church building could be constructed within view of the emperor's palace in the capital shows not only that Christianity was rapidly growing, but that it also had a strong emphasis on dedicated space for worship. Otherwise, it would have been doubtful that a building would have existed that was large enough to hold the entire congregation at the same time.

Church Buildings after Constantine

The Edict of Milan in AD 313 made Christianity legal, and Constantine's ascension to the throne changed everything. Once Christianity could step into the light of day without any fear of future persecution, church construction moved forward at a rapid pace. Elements that may or may not have been a part of a congregational understanding of a theology of architecture now became commonplace. More often than not, the basilica model was retained, but now uniquely Christian features became regular. A basilica was just a large lecture hall. It was a room with a high ceiling, supported by columns running the length of it. Most church buildings were constructed facing west, which re-created the orientation of the temple in Jerusalem. A few centuries later the orientation was flipped, and most church buildings were then constructed facing east, though the construction was still based on the temple.

Because the temple was divided into different sections, church buildings were divided into different sections. Perhaps this was common before the legalization of Christianity, but archaeological evidence is scant. From the house church in Dura-Europos to this new construction, more and more ornamental and ceremonial construction was included to reinforce the perception that Christian worship was a fulfillment (and in some sense a continuation) of the worship God instituted for the temple and perfected in Jesus Christ's high priesthood. Gone was the single room for the congregation to gather. Now there was a new creation, the *templon*. This new architectural feature was a low barrier that separated the worship space into two distinct areas. One, which was smaller and contained the altar for the sacrament, was called the *sanctuary*. The other, which was larger and for the worshiping congregation, was called the *nave*. The templon was a solid construction, usually of stone, that was approximately knee-high. Often it also had columns that rose above it to the ceiling, or at least there was a canopy over the sanctuary area. Between these columns curtains could be hung, and in many congregations those curtains were closed at certain points in the service. This closed off the sanctuary from the nave, usually during portions of the Eucharist service. That the templon was introduced as an imitation of the temple is corroborated by the presence of templa (the plural of templon) in synagogues of the same era as the Torah screen. Both the Jewish and the Christian communities created worship spaces based on the record of the temple layout in Jerusalem.

As time continued, the templon grew larger. In the East, it became what is today known as the *iconostasis*. This is the wall of icons that separated the sanctuary from the nave in Orthodox and Eastern Catholic church buildings. In the West, it became the *rood screen*, a lattice or wrought-iron screen that separated the altar from the rest of the congregation. This is why what is known as the sanctuary in the East is often called the chancel in the West. *Chancel* comes from the Latin word *cancellus*, which means "lattice." After the Reformation, many of the rood screens were cut down or removed in Protestant churches. In Roman Catholic churches, they were removed as well, and in their place a low railing was installed, variously called a chancel railing, an altar railing, or a communion railing. Ironically, the altar railing brought church architecture back to the more ancient templon, but without the curtains to completely separate the chancel from the congregation.

Equally ironic, the altar railing, so common in Protestant church buildings, was a feature of the Roman Catholic Counter-Reformation.

The altar was another development in Christian architecture that changed during this period of time and subsequently. Before the legalization of Christianity, the church would celebrate the Eucharist in various places, such as house churches or in catacombs. There is very little evidence for what the requirements were for the surface on which the sacrament was celebrated. However, once the period of the imperial church began, there was much information as to what a proper altar should be. Initially, the preferred location of the altar was in the sanctuary/chancel area as a free-standing table. It was not supposed to be against a wall or affixed to one. When the church buildings were designed facing west, this allowed the priest or bishop to move behind the table and face east while celebrating the sacrament. There is some indication that the entire congregation would face east during this portion of the service in some worshiping communities. All of those gathered would turn and face the eastern end of the building as the priest continued the service. Another factor that necessitated the free-standing table was that the celebrant was supposed to be able to encircle it while using a censer at specific points during services. This is still the practice of the Eastern churches today.

At some point in the West, after the orientation of the church building was flipped to face east, the altar table was affixed to the eastern wall. When this happened, the priest or bishop remained facing east during the celebration of the service. This effectively made the priest have his back to the congregation throughout the majority of the service. The reason for facing east during the Eucharist was twofold. First, the priests in the temple would face east when making the sacrifices for the people. If Christian worship was a fulfillment of Jewish temple worship and a continuation of it through the high priesthood of Christ, it would only be natural that the Christian offering would be made facing the same way. Second, it was so that nature itself could help reinforce the reality of worship. If one of the main points of the incarnation, crucifixion, and resurrection of Christ was that the darkness could not overcome the light, then it was good practice to face the coming of the dawn as the believers gathered for worship, seeing the first rays of light shining through the darkness. As the role of the priest became more defined as the one who led worship on behalf of the people, and there was no need for the priest to walk around the table any longer in the Western liturgy, it became highly logical to fix the table to the eastern wall. If, as in the temple, the further to one end one goes, the holier the space, then the altar on which Christ is present in the Eucharist ought to be at the farthest point possible toward the holy end of the building.

The farthest point in the building, the place where the Eucharist should be, would then be the high altar. This was the main altar upon which the normal Sunday service would be celebrated. It would not only be on the farthest end of the building, but in many ways it would also be the focal point of the entire worship space. This was to draw everyone's eyes to that which was considered most important in worship. In later construction, especially in large parishes and cathedrals, there would also be side altars and chapels in different places throughout the church building. The main reason for the side altars was the idea that only one Mass should be celebrated on an altar in any twenty-four-hour period. By having more than one altar in a church building, more than one mass could take place.

In both East and West, the altar tables also contained relics from particular saints. It is not clear in the historical record exactly why this practice began or when it became required, but to this day for a Roman Catholic or Eastern Orthodox altar to be a properly consecrated altar for worship, it must contain a relic of a saint. Many believe this practice goes back to the time when Christians worshiped in the catacombs, using the tombs or niches of the saints for the flat surface on which the Communion elements were set. There is a scriptural reference to saints under the altar in heaven in Revelation 6:9. Nevertheless, the exact reason this practice was introduced is not known.

With the Reformation, altar tables were pulled off of the wall and placed more toward the people once again. Relics were removed, ornate tables destroyed, and the entire piece of furniture was re-designated as a Communion Table.[1] The term *altar* was abandoned because of the sacrificial sound of it and to counter the prevailing notion that each Mass was a re-sacrifice of Jesus. Clergy moved behind the table once again, and they faced the congregation as they proceeded through their service. This was done to further move away from the perceived sacrificial nature of the sacrament in Roman Catholic practice of the day. The minister was not a priest standing before the people, making an offering. Rather, the minister was a fellow believer who invited the people to commune with God and one another at the Communion Table.

Another interesting architectural feature of church buildings was seating for the congregation. There was none. Again, this was a continuation of worship in the temple, where there were no seats for the worshipers. Even in the earliest house churches, this would logically be the case, as there were no such thing as folding chairs for the entire congregation to use. People stood, knelt, or sat on the floor during worship. In the earliest days of the church, the most appropriate posture during worship was to stand. This was because it was a celebration of Christ's victory over sin and death, and because Christians believed that in their worship God was in their midst. If the Ruler of the universe was there, the most appropriate posture would be to stand in God's presence just as one would do for the emperor. As church buildings became larger, seating was still not installed. This allowed the congregation to move about during the service. If a particular worshiper wanted to pray, or walk on a "pilgrimage" around the holy relics in the building, or show children the various images throughout the building, he or she was free to so do. Seats did not appear for the congregation

---

1 Many people also used the term *the Lord's Table*, although this is actually a common Roman Catholic term for the altar as well.

until shortly before the Reformation, and even then, the church buildings that did have them were few and far between. Most older cathedrals in Europe and other traditionally Christian areas still have very few seats for the congregation. Even today, Eastern Orthodox congregations often do not have congregational seating.

Congregational seating became nearly universal after the Reformation. This was because the focus of the worship service was on the preaching and teaching portion. The worshiper's role looked more and more like the role of a student in a lecture; therefore, it was necessary for congregants to be seated so they could learn. However, this introduction of congregational seating, pews specifically, actually worked against one of the main tenets of the Reformation. At a time when the emphasis was on recapturing the notion of the priesthood of all believers and that worship was not merely observing someone *do* worship on behalf of the entire congregation, the introduction of seats turned the average congregation member into more of a passive spectator during worship than before. It also had an unintended consequence of reinforcing social stratification. Before there were fixed seats in a church building, the space was open and people were, at least architecturally, on the same level. Anyone could stand anywhere or move anywhere. Once fixed seating was introduced, those who could afford the best seats in the house purchased or rented them. This was common practice for a long time. If a person or family could not afford decent seating, they were reminded of that fact every time they worshiped God. It was very much akin to the situation in Corinth when celebrating the Lord's Supper where the class distinctions were reinforced rather than broken down in the fellowship meal, as recorded in 1 Corinthians 11:17-22. It was not until approximately three hundred years after the introduction of pews in church buildings that they also became free for any and all people to use. This is a good warning for those involved in liturgical change today. Many times the solution to one issue that seems perfectly logical and useful can unintentionally create new issues that need to be solved. This is part of the reason the adage is true: *ecclesia semper reformanda*, the church is always reforming (or, the church is always in need of reform).

The general style of architecture underwent several different modifications from the original basilica design over time as well. Some of these changes were due to practical considerations; some were theological in nature. Some, like the proliferation of side altars in churches, were both practical and theological. In the eastern portion of the empire, the dome became a standard symbol of a church building. Large icons were painted on the walls and ceiling, to evoke the sense that heaven was descending to earth. The icons were primarily based on an Egyptian style of art that commemorated deceased loved ones. Christians adapted the practice and used it to paint pictures of Christ, biblical figures, saints, and scenes from the Bible or the history of the church, and put them in as many places within the church building as possible. The theology behind using images was twofold. First, because God took on a physical form so that humanity could comprehend the incomprehensible, it was logical that the church could use physical images to help its members understand their own history and faith. This was actually the decision of the Seventh Ecumenical Council, held in Nicea in 787.

Second, worship was a fulfillment and continuation of Jewish worship. That being the case, Christians looked to the design of the tabernacle and temple for guidance in decorating their worship spaces. In Exodus 36 the Israelites were instructed to make the tabernacle, receiving great detail from God how it should look. One of the key pieces of decoration were the curtains that surrounded it. These were the walls of this mobile temple. They were blue, purple, and crimson, and they had cherubim woven into them. In addition, the ark of the covenant also had cherubim on its lid. The theology that was to be taught by these images was that when one entered into the tabernacle, that person stepped out of the ordinary world and into the place where heaven and earth met. Because cherubim were in heaven, they were in the worship space of the tabernacle. This imagery was later carried over into Solomon's temple. Here, cherubim were also carved into all the walls and embroidered in the curtains, and there were two giant statues of cherubim that stood in front of the Holy of Holies. Again, the theological idea was that this space was different from the rest of the world. It was the dwelling place of God.

Because Christianity inherited this understanding from Judaism, it is only natural that Christians continued it in worship. As noted earlier, even the earliest church building, Dura-Europos, had iconography all over its walls, and the only way to tell the church building apart from the synagogue a few streets away was by which stories were painted on the walls.

As time moved forward, more and more saints began appearing in iconography alongside biblical images and stories. This was because of the Christian understanding of heaven. If one died in Christ, that person was immediately with Christ. This idea came from several different places in Scripture, none the least of which were Jesus saying to the thief on the cross, "Truly I tell you, today you will be with me in Paradise" in Luke 23:43, and Paul's statement in Philippians 1:23, "My desire is to depart and be with Christ." Given this understanding, it was only natural that these Christians would put icons of those faithful Christian witnesses on the walls of their buildings. If the church building was a place where heaven and earth met, someplace different from the rest of the world, then it is right and fitting that they had images of Christians on the walls they were sure were in heaven.

However, these images were never intended to be objects of worship. Their design, from the beginning, was to be a visual Bible, a means of instruction, and a means of encouragement for the faithful. This was still centuries before most people had access to a copy of the Bible, and when much of the population was semiliterate at best. Visual imagery became a key mode of teaching for the vast majority of the church. As well, seeing images of those who had successfully run the race of faith and gained the victor's crown was a way of making real the great cloud of witnesses in Hebrews 11 and 12. It was also a reminder that the Christian life was possible and it was encouraging and motivating to see people who actually did it, and being surrounded by these images reminded worshipers that they had a large Christian family praying for their faithfulness.

In the West, architecture and decoration took a different turn. Rather than use domes as a way to visualize heaven coming down to earth, the constructional motif was to seek ways to reach higher and higher from earth to heaven. Over the centuries designs and building technology developed so that as people walked into a church building, their eyes and their spirits were lifted up into the heavenly realms. This difference between Eastern and Western church design is a perfect example of *lex orandi, lex credendi*. During the Eucharistic portion of the worship service, the Eastern liturgical tradition had what is called an *epiclesis*, a prayer that asks God to descend and pour out the Holy Spirit on the gifts offered and the people present. The Western liturgical tradition did not have the epiclesis as a part of its prayers. In the East, the people were taught in prayer and architecture that God descended to them. In the West, the people were taught in prayer and architecture to "lift up your hearts" unto the Lord.

Another difference between East and West was the nature of the images used in worship. The East almost exclusively used icons, flat painted images. The West used statuary, three-dimensional images to convey similar goals of teaching and edification. Even though these images were obviously statues, this was never understood as idolatry because the church made a distinction between worship and veneration. Worship is only due to God. Veneration is having a sense of respect toward something religious. It would be analogous today to how some congregations place a large Bible on their Communion tables. It is venerated, not worshiped. The Christian leaders and theologians who developed the practice and theology of using images in worship, both flat icons and statues, were well aware of the commandments not to worship graven images and idols. They made a clear distinction between worship and veneration. Unfortunately, those to whom they were supposed to teach that distinction did not always understand it. Just as the Israelites began to worship the bronze serpent created by Moses in the wilderness and offer incense to it (Numbers 21:4-9; 2 Kings 18:4), so too many Christians worshiped the images, paintings, or statues, as if they contained the identity of the characters depicted. This was the reason for the iconoclastic fervor of many of the Reformers. Hezekiah destroyed the bronze serpent, and likewise, many of the statues in church buildings were destroyed in the sixteenth century.

Because of the Reformation, not only was imagery removed from church buildings, but the design of the buildings changed as well. Whereas the design of the worship space was created to emulate the temple's design, and the architecture was intentionally developed to convey the mystery of corporate worship with the parishioner being lifted up to heaven in spirit, Protestantism took a decidedly different approach. Now the focus was not on an encounter between heaven and earth, usually typified in the sacrament, but rather it was on the transfer of biblical truth through the reading of Scripture and the exposition of those readings by delivering sermons. Worship became less about an incomprehensible theological mystery in the sacrament and more about a way to teach people knowledge of the Bible. Because of this transformation and difference in emphasis, Protestant church buildings began to look more like meeting houses or lecture rooms in a university. The pulpit was made the center and focal point of the room, because the sermon became the center and focal point of the service. This was the common form for Protestant church buildings until the Liturgical Movement of the nineteenth and twentieth centuries, when Protestants began looking at the history of worship. Because of this rediscovery of the history of worship, many realigned their services to incorporate more of an emphasis on the sacramental aspect of worship. This, in turn, led to a different way of designing church buildings. Many facilities constructed after this point intentionally put the pulpit to one side of the chancel area and placed the Communion Table in the middle as the focal point once again. The table itself began to be called alternatively a communion table or an altar. Interior furnishings became more ornate, and the simple, lecture room feel was changed.

Not all Protestant congregations, fellowships, or denominations embraced the Liturgical Movement, however. Many, prompted by the seeker-sensitive expressions of worship created in the 1970s, moved further away from even a traditional Protestant form of worship. Architecturally, these church buildings were designed more as auditoriums or multipurpose buildings. The emphasis moved from the Protestant focus on delivering biblical truth to keeping the community engaged in what was happening in the front of the building. Chancel areas began to look more and more like stages. If the central focal point in a Roman Catholic church building was the altar, and the center focal point in a traditional Protestant church building was the pulpit, in these new-style church buildings the center focal point was the music. The major emphasis in the service moved from the mystery of heaven and earth meeting in the sacrament (Roman Catholic), to the conveying of biblical truth (traditional Protestant), to emotional engagement through music.

This leads to an important point in the design and decoration of any worship space: the space itself communicates theology. This communication can be intentional or unintentional, but where things are placed, what items are used, the order in which they are used, and the care with which they are used all communicate something about that congregation's understanding of who God is, who they are in relation to God, and how the interaction between them and God happens. Because human beings take in information through a variety of senses, each one of those senses contributes to the overall message being communicated. This means that a person who, upon entering a particular church building's worship space for the first time, can get a general understanding of what is most important to that particular congregation based on what draws the most visual attention. This may or may not be the message that congregation wishes to communicate, but it does happen. In the three examples above, each of them conveys a different theological truth based on what is the focal point of the space. The first is union with God. The second is truth about God. The third is feeling about God and one another. Those three also convey the main focus of the worship experience. The first is the mystery of God. The second is the need for right understanding about God. The third is participants' response to God.

This kind of theological reflection on design and function is not limited to what is most visible within a church building either. It can be applied to other parts of the facility. How large the lobby (narthex/vestibule) is communicates how much emphasis on fellowship of the worshiping community there is in the congregation. If not much space is set aside for interpersonal interactions beyond the worship area, it rightly or wrongly communicates that fellowship is not a priority for that congregation. How the seating for the congregation in the worship space is arranged also communicates. If there are multiple aisles and space between rows of seats for movement, it communicates the expectation that there will be movement in the service. Either people will move in place as they worship or they are free to move to different locations within the worship space—forward for prayer or Communion, to greet other people, or to seek out others who may need prayer and comfort. If there are narrow rows with few aisles, it communicates that the people are spectators, who find their seats and remain there throughout the service. That may not be the intended message a particular congregation wants to communicate, but it is the practical reality that exists.

Essentially, for a worshiping congregation to communicate a coherent and unified message in worship, even the architecture and decoration of the church building must be considered. Many congregations do not have the luxury of building a new facility and must do the best they can with the building they have to communicate the message they desire. This is where the furnishings and layout within the building become important. Every person or team that is responsible for worship ought to take time to ask one simple question of themselves:

What is the purpose for worship? Once that question is answered, the follow-up question is: What would it look like in our community if we accomplished what we desired in worship? Then the next question is: How do we design our church building to help facilitate those results? Use the theology of worship for that congregation in that community to dictate what the sacred space should be and have. In this way, even the "rocks" of the church building will cry out God's message to the world.

4

THE ORDER OF WORSHIP

People are absolutely necessary for Christian worship. It is, after all, the work of the people. Space is also an important element in worship. Sacred space that is set apart from the rest of everyday life may not be essential, but it communicates the holy is distinct from the common. Having a dedicated space for worship allows people to tangibly experience the uniqueness of encountering the living God together.

Another aspect to Christian worship that is absolutely essential is an order for worship. This is true because God is a God of order, not chaos. God created order from chaos. All things are to be done orderly in church (1 Corinthians 14:33). This is not to say that every single congregation throughout the entire world must have the same elements in worship in the same sequence on the same day, but if it is Christian worship, there will be a basic pattern to worship that congregations follow. The language metaphor works well here. There are certain rules for grammar that make a sentence correct. Some sentences are more complex than others, and some are longer than others. Yet if a sentence is grammatically correct, no matter the length or complexity, it follows the same rules. This principle holds true for Christian worship. The nouns of worship (persons, places, things) and the verbs of worship (actions) all fit into a basic grammatical rule for the gathering to be truly Christian and truly worship. No matter how short or long, simple or complex, the same story is told with the same pattern.

The Basic Pattern

The starting place for Christian worship is God. Revelation 22:13 states, "I am the Alpha and the Omega, the first and the last, the beginning and the end." Everything finds its origin and its completion in God. With that concept in the background of the discussion, it is possible to look at the basic pattern of worship. The basic pattern for worship is a twofold movement of drawing near to God and God drawing near to us. This is illustrated in James 4:8, "Draw near to God, and he will draw near to you." These two verses together, from Revelation and James, give the basic pattern for Christian worship. Behind the scenes, as it were, God first moves toward us in prevenient grace. God is always the initiator in our saving relationship and every step we take closer to God is always in response to the grace already given to us. This movement in the basic pattern does not necessarily have to happen within the context of worship. A person may be prompted to seek out Christians to worship their God because of an experience of grace that was quite apart from the church. Someone may witness signs or wonders, natural or supernatural, in the world and be drawn to Jesus Christ. Jesus himself may appear to people, as happens quite regularly in certain areas of the world today, and direct people to seek out Christians and the church. A conversation with a coworker may be a catalyst to help a person experience God's grace in his or her life. Whatever the means, God's grace is the first movement in worship.

With that in mind, in worship, first, we draw near to God. We reach up toward heaven as the people God has called from every tribe, nation, language, and race upon the earth. Worship is a response by the people to the grace they have received from God. In Wesleyan theology this may be prevenient grace, convicting grace, justifying grace, or even sanctifying grace. The response of the people to that grace is worship, drawing near to God. One major implication of this fact is that worship services are not evangelistic in nature or outreach-focused; although that may be an outcome. Worship is God-focused, as it is humans' response to what God has done and is doing in their lives. This means that when a service is planned with the focus on the people, it is not worship. Evangelism is necessary in the life of the church, but it is not worship. People may have a greater experience of God's grace during a worship service, and that should be the case; but the primary focus is not a first-time introduction to God's grace for people who have never had an experience of God in their lives before that moment. Worship is a response to what has already happened in someone's life. This does not exclude the possibility of someone first coming to faith in a worship service, but it does mean that the focus and goal of the service is not on facilitating that kind of a response in those who are not yet believers. When that happens, it is usually a person responding to the prevenient grace God has given her or him already, and that is a beautiful event. God willing, this would happen in many worship services, but the distinction between a worship service and an evangelistic service still needs to be understood. One is intentionally God-focused while the other is intentionally people-focused. A healthy congregation will have both in its corporate life.

The second movement is God's. Because God moved in people's lives (knowingly or unknowingly), and because people responded to that grace and have drawn near, now God comes to them once again more fully. People draw near to God, and then God draws near to them. This is God's response to those who "call upon the name of the Lord." This means that the pattern is divine action–human response–divine action. In the actual human response of calling upon the Lord and drawing near to God and then God's response of drawing near to people, there is a trinitarian form at work.

First, heaven and earth meet. During a worship service, the congregation becomes an outpost of the kingdom of God. The new creation is being revealed in the life of the community. As Paul wrote in 2 Corinthians 5:17, "So, if anyone is in Christ, there is a new creation." When the community that represents that new creation gathers together, the idea becomes a reality. No longer is it a gathering of people with similar experiences or like-minded purposes, as any other human gathering of a club or institution. Instead, the congregation becomes a signpost for the reign of God on earth as in heaven. As such, the creator of both realms is acknowledged, worshiped, and glorified as Creator and God.

Second, because the church is the body of Christ, every time the church gathers together, it participates in the Incarnation. Worship becomes a mystical event every time it happens, but not in an esoteric way. It becomes mystical in a very real way. Christ's body is enthroned in heaven, yet the church is his body on earth. When a congregation of members of that body gather together, there is a representation of the body of Christ once again on earth. This means that every worship service is miraculous, as Jesus shows up once again in the midst of his people. Jesus told the disciples that "where two or three are gathered in my name, I am there among them" (Matthew 18:20). Each time the people gather together, it is an experience of the risen Christ in their midst and it is a reminder to the world of the reality of the gospel message.

Finally, when there is Christian worship, the people have an encounter with the living God. This is because the church is not only the body of Christ, but it is also the temple of the Holy Spirit. Each Christian is a "living stone" being built into this new temple, the place where God dwells on earth. When the people then gather together for worship, the presence of the Holy Spirit fills the assembly and indwells the people. As the people draw near to God, God draws near to them. This is done as the Creator of a new creation, the body of Christ, and the indwelling of the Holy Spirit into the temple. This is the basic pattern for Christian worship. This is the order, the proper grammar, which all Christian worship ought to follow. Which elements, which nouns and verbs, have been included in different times and different places to embody that basic pattern can be different, but they all adhere to this grammar if they are properly Christian worship.

Biblical Worship

One of the greatest frustrations for scholars in trying to see how the early church worshiped is that there is no place in the Bible that spells out what happened during a worship service. Instead, scholars have had to cobble together a picture of what worship might have been from snippets and inferences. The problem inherent with this process is that the biblical texts themselves come from different times and different places. In bringing them all together to form a composite of biblical worship and declaring that the resulting picture is how the early church worshiped, the underlying assumption is that all churches throughout the Roman Empire at all times during the first century worshiped the same way. This is a false assumption. Simply looking at the life of the church in Acts and in Corinth would lead to the conclusion that not all Christians in all places and all times had the same worship. In Acts, the believers met together every day in homes. In Corinth, the believers met together less frequently. In Acts, the believers gave everything they owned to the apostles as a part of their worship and fellowship so the entire community would have its needs met. In Corinth, there were rich believers and poor believers, and one of the causes of division within that community was the lack of compassion and sharing between the two. Even within Acts itself, there are at least two different images of worship. In chapter 2, the believers met every day in homes to break bread. By chapter 20, the believers met on the first day of the week to break bread. Biblical worship was not uniform across time and space. The best we can do by bringing all of the biblical accounts together in a composite is to see what seeds were present in various communities. It will be out of these seeds that worship grew and developed.

All of this means that it is possible to lift out of the New Testament glimpses of worship by the Christian community. Yet it must be remembered that these glimpses may have been local or more widespread in scope. They may have been time-bound or continued. They may have been representative of the church throughout the empire, or they may have been unique to one particular worshiping community. In addition, there are several different founders (or at least theological influencers) of the various worshiping communities described in the Bible. Because of these facts, the assumption of this book at this early stage of development in worship is that while the Holy Spirit may have guided the church into all truth (John 16:13), and those theological truths may have taken different forms and shapes in different locations and over different time periods, they may have developed at different rates of time.

An appropriate analogy may be a photograph of a third-grade class. Each of the individual students has his or her own unique characteristics, yet they are all in the third grade together. They attend the same school, learn the same subjects, have the same school experiences, and are guided by the same teacher. Each of these faces, however, will assimilate the information in different ways. Some will more quickly grasp some materials than others. Some will learn at different rates than others. All will grow in ways unique to themselves. This is true of the New Testament worshiping communities. They are all Christian congregations, indwelt with the Holy Spirit, but they do not all look the same or sound the same. With that in mind, it is possible to look at the biblical texts for worship and see the seeds of later worship.

Acts 1

In the first chapter of Acts, the believers were gathered together and "constantly devoting themselves to prayer" (1:14). While this protracted prayer meeting happens, Peter delivered a short message that included a scriptural reference, response to a current situation, and an opportunity for concrete action and response. This snippet of scripture shows the community in prayer, exposition on biblical texts, and an opportunity for the entire community to respond.

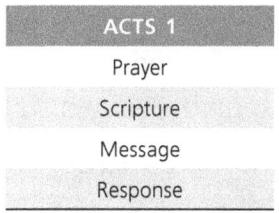

Acts 2

At the end of Peter's speech on Pentecost, there is a description of what those first Christians did as they gathered together. First, in response to Peter's evangelistic call to repent and return to God, the people who responded were baptized. Then, they "devoted themselves to the apostles' teaching and fellowship, to the breaking of bread and the prayers" (Acts 2:42). Here is another short vignette of scripture that gives a basic formula for worship. Interestingly, these four elements, teaching, fellowship, breaking of bread, prayers, will become the basic skeleton for later worship even up to today. It is very similar to what happened before Pentecost and is a logical continuation of that group meeting together.

Of these four elements, five if one counts baptism of the new converts, one has an exact correspondence with the actions of the believers in chapter 1, prayer. The apostles' teaching could conceivably be equated with scripture and a message concerning that scripture. It would be from the scriptural texts that the community would later disciple its newest members to understand just who Jesus is and how his life, death, resurrection, and ascension are the fulfillment of the promises made to Israel through its prophets. It would be similar to the teaching Jesus took on the road to Emmaus in Luke 24 with two disciples as he "interpreted to them the things about himself in all the scriptures" (24:27). The response in chapter 1 was to a specific call, namely, determining who Judas's replacement would be. The breaking of bread, both in its sacramental implications as Holy Communion and as an ordinary meal, as well as the fellowship, are not responses in the same way. There is not a neat correspondence between these aspects of worship. This leaves two different glimpses into what the earliest Christians did when they gathered together for worship:

ACTS 1	ACTS 2
	Baptism
Prayer	Prayer
Scripture	Apostles' Teaching
Message	Apostles' Teaching
Response	
	Breaking Bread
	Fellowship

Acts 20

Toward the end of Acts, there is a very brief statement, "On the first day of the week, when we met to break bread . . ." (20:7). Two instances stand out in this one verse. First, while the earliest Christians met every day in homes and in the temple while the movement resided exclusively in Jerusalem (Acts 2), now the people met on the first day of the week. This was a shift in meeting from every day to one day, and it was even a shift from the one day holy to Jewish tradition, the Sabbath (Saturday), to the day on which Jesus was resurrected, the First Day (Sunday). Second, the believers here gathered to break bread.

There is some debate concerning this phrase that Luke uses. There is evidence that it could mean the sacrament of the Lord's Supper, and there is evidence that it means a simple meal. This book takes the former meaning as most plausible. This would mean that the Christian worship described here in Acts 20 was on Sunday and had the Lord's Supper as a regular part of its order. There was also the somewhat humorous scene here of Eutychus falling asleep as Paul spoke to the group assembled. Hopefully this did not mean that boring, long, drawn-out preaching was an element of this worship!

ACTS 1	ACTS 2	ACTS 20
		Sunday
	Baptism	
Prayer	Prayer	
Scripture	Apostles' teaching	
Message	Apostles' teaching	Message
Response		
	Breaking bread	Breaking bread
	Fellowship	

1 Corinthians 11

Some of the most interesting biblical texts for worship come from 1 Corinthians. This is because so much of what was happening in Corinth in worship was wrong that Paul had to write correctives to the problems. In chapter 11, Paul detailed a scene where the congregation gathered together to celebrate the Lord's Supper, but according to Paul they were all wrong in their approach to the situation and the sacrament. Interestingly, at this point in the life of the Corinthian congregation it seemed that the sacrament was not completely separate from a meal that the entire congregation ate together. Unlike potluck or pitch-in dinners in many congregations today, however, each family brought their own food and ate their own food. At some point, either during this meal or after it, the sacrament itself was celebrated. Here is where there is the most interest for liturgical development today, as the words of institution were already set. The words Jesus spoke as he inaugurated the sacrament were delivered, with slight variation from what is in the Gospels, intact by Paul to Corinth. This is the earliest written account of the Lord's Supper, as the composition of 1 Corinthians predates the composition of the Gospels by at least ten years, and it was written by someone who was neither in the upper room with Jesus nor noted to be a companion of anyone who was in the upper room.[1]

1 Corinthians 14

Unfortunately for Paul, but fortunately for posterity, problems at the Lord's Supper were not the only issues in Corinth. In fact, worship there was fairly raucous, if Paul accurately described the situation he attempted to correct.

> What should be done then, my friends? When you come together, each one has a hymn, a lesson, a revelation, a tongue, or an interpretation. Let all things be done for building up. If anyone speaks in a tongue, let there be only two or at most three, and each in turn; and let one interpret. But if there is no one to interpret, let them be silent in church and speak to themselves and to God. Let two or three prophets speak, and let the others weigh what is said. If a revelation is made to someone else sitting nearby, let the first person be silent. For you can all prophesy one by one, so that all may learn and all be encouraged. (14:26-31).

Here was an attempt to correct what must have been a complete cacophony when it comes to worship. There were multiple people trying to speak or sing. There were multiple lessons and revelations from God. From the image of the description, it seems as if everyone was trying to be heard by the community all at once. It is into this situation that Paul tried to carve out order from chaos.

ACTS 1	ACTS 2	ACTS 20	1 CORINTHIANS
		Sunday	
	Baptism		

---

[1] Matthew was one of the original apostles present in the upper room, and according to tradition, Mark recorded Peter's teachings as what we now know as his Gospel. Luke unapologetically stated that he was not an eyewitness to Jesus's ministry, but that he interviewed people who were. Paul had none of these connections, but had brief encounters with the earliest Christians in Jerusalem after his conversion.

ACTS 1	ACTS 2	ACTS 20	1 CORINTHIANS
			Hymns
Prayer	Prayer		
			Revelations
			Tongues
Scripture	Apostles' teaching		
Message	Apostles' teaching	Message	Lessons
Response			
	Breaking bread	Breaking bread	Lord's Supper
	Fellowship		
			Dinner

1 Thessalonians 5

One of Paul's earlier letters, 1 Thessalonians, has a short snippet that gave a very cursory look at what the Christians in Thessalonica did when they gathered together in worship.

> But we appeal to you, brothers and sisters, to respect those who labor among you, and have charge of you in the Lord and admonish you; esteem them very highly in love because of their work. Be at peace among yourselves. And we urge you, beloved, to admonish the idlers, encourage the faint hearted, help the weak, be patient with all of them. See that none of you repays evil for evil, but always seek to do good to one another and to all. Rejoice always, pray without ceasing, give thanks in all circumstances; for this is the will of God in Christ Jesus for you. Do not quench the Spirit. Do not despise the words of prophets, but test everything; hold fast to what is good. (5:12-21)

This passage shows that there were leaders in the congregation who had responsibility for teaching and correction among the people there. What is interesting in this fact is that, as far as history and tradition are concerned, no traveling companion of Paul's was left in Thessalonica.

This means that before the missionary team left the city, leaders were appointed and placed over the congregation. Whether that included what could be construed as ordination in any sense of the word is not known, but some Christians were set apart for leadership. As well, there was prayer and prophecy in Thessalonica, and with regard to the prophecy, there was also a call to test the prophecies. Who exactly was empowered to test these prophecies is not told, and it may have been the responsibility of the entire congregation since the letter was addressed to all of them.

ACTS 1	ACTS 2	ACTS 20	1 CORINTHIANS	1 THESSALONIANS
				Leaders
		Sunday		
	Baptism			
			Hymns	
Prayer	Prayer			Prayer
			Revelations	Prophecies
			Tongues	
Scripture	Apostles' teaching			
Message	Apostles' teaching	Message	Lessons	
Response				Testing prophecies
	Breaking bread	Breaking bread	Lord's Supper	
	Fellowship			
			Dinner	

Hebrews 10

Hebrews is very different in tone and scope from many of the other books in the New Testament. Regarding worship, this is no exception. There are several places in Hebrews that could be lifted out as an example of its language concerning Christians as they gathered together, but this passage from chapter 10 is axiomatic for the work.

> Therefore, my friends, since we have confidence to enter the sanctuary by the blood of Jesus, by the new and living way that he opened for us through the curtain (that is, through his flesh), and since we have a great priest over the house of God, let us approach with a true heart in full assurance of faith, with our hearts sprinkled clean from an evil conscience and our bodies washed with pure water. Let us hold fast to the confession of our hope without wavering, for he who has promised is faithful. And let us consider how to provoke one another to love and good deeds, not neglecting to meet together, as is the habit of some, but encouraging one another, and all the more as you see the Day approaching. (10:19-25)

The first piece to notice from this passage is its use of temple and sacrifice imagery when speaking of gathering together. Jesus was equated with a priest, the high priest elsewhere in the book, and images of curtains, a sanctuary, the sprinkling of blood and washing of water all pointed to imagery of the sacrificial and priestly system of worship given by God on Mount Sinai to Moses and embodied in the temple in Jerusalem.

The second item of interest in this passage is the encouragement to continue meeting together as a church. This is interesting for two main reasons: (a) it had to be said, which means that people were dropping off from meeting together, and (b) the author saw it as intrinsic to the success of living the Christian life to gather together on a regular basis. Evidently, the community to which Hebrews was originally addressed had a problem with people no longer seeing the need to gather together as the church. The book of Hebrews was written to remedy that. What is most fascinating about this issue, though, is that it becomes obvious that meeting together as the church was not just important to Luke or to Paul but was also included as a necessity by this author as well. There is no indication as to the frequency, duration, or location of the meeting, but the corporate gathering of the church is understood to be vital here.

ACTS 1	ACTS 2	ACTS 20	1 CORINTHIANS	1 THESSALONIANS	HEBREWS
					Temple language
				Leaders	
		Sunday			
	Baptism				
			Hymns		
Prayer	Prayer				Prayer
			Revelation	Prophecy	
			Tongues		
Scripture	Apostles' teaching				
Message	Apostles' teaching	Message	Lessons		
Response				Testing prophecy	
	Breaking bread	Breaking bread	Lord's Supper		
	Fellowship				
			Dinner		Meeting together

James 5

All of the biblical accounts thus far could potentially be connected to Paul. There were several statements from Paul himself, and there were several statements from Luke in Acts. Since Luke was a traveling companion of Paul, and since Luke is self-identified as having to learn his understanding of the faith from others (having not been among the original apostles or disciples), the case could be made that Luke's concept of the faith and how it is to be lived in people's lives was taught to him by Paul. This connects Acts to Paul. The author of Hebrews is, to paraphrase Origen in the 200s, known only to God, yet there is a long tradition of associating the letter with Paul. This means a case could be made, even if it is a long shot, that Hebrews is connected to Paul. This next passage is, therefore, the first uncontestably independent witness in the biblical understanding of worship.

James was the brother of Jesus and very much a Jewish Christian. Whereas much of Paul's writings revolved around how Jews and Gentiles together could worship God as revealed in Jesus Christ, James wrote from a Jewish perspective to Jewish believers in Jesus. From both church tradition and the writings of Josephus, the portrait of James that takes shape is one of a man who was so full of devotion that both Jewish followers of Jesus and Jewish nonbelievers in Jesus recognized him as righteous and just. James wrote concerning Christian gatherings in 5:13-16:

> Are any among you suffering? They should pray. Are any cheerful? They should sing songs of praise. Are any among you sick? They should call for the elders of the church and have them pray over them, anointing them with oil in the name of the Lord. The prayer of faith will save the sick, and the Lord will raise them up; and anyone who has committed sins will be forgiven. Therefore confess your sins to one another, and pray for one another, so that you may be healed. The prayer of the righteous is powerful and effective.

This discourse may or may not have been concerning actual worship practices in their original setting. Nevertheless, these became a part of worship in the years following the letter. It may be an example of healing miracles within the church, or it may be that the healing referred to was not physical but rather spiritual in nature since it was embedded within a discussion on forgiveness of sins. Either way, this is an example of Christians being encouraged to not only pray and sing, but to anoint one another with oil, physically pray for one another, and to confess to one another in order to be forgiven by one another.

ACTS 1	ACTS 2	ACTS 20	1 CORINTHIANS	1 THESSALONIANS	HEBREWS	JAMES
					Temple language	
				Leaders		
		Sunday				
	Baptism					
			Hymns			Songs of praise
Prayer	Prayer			Prayer		Prayer
						Laying on of hands
						Anointing with oil
			Revelation	Prophecy		
			Tongues			
Scripture	Apostles' teaching					
Message	Apostles' teaching	Message	Lessons			
Response				Testing prophecy		
	Breaking bread	Breaking bread	Lord's Supper			
	Fellowship					
						Confession
			Dinner		Meeting together	

1 Peter

Peter's first epistle has two short sections that give glimpses into the gathering of the early church. The first is 4:10-11:

> Like good stewards of the manifold grace of God, serve one another with whatever gift each of you has received. Whoever speaks must do so as one speaking the very words of God; whoever serves must do so with the strength that God supplies, so that God may be glorified in all things through Jesus Christ.

Like the list of gifts that Paul gave in his letters, and like the usage of gifts for the edification of the believers that James insinuated, Peter briefly described a situation in which certain believers within the church had gifts from God that were to be used confidently for the benefit of the church.

The second passage that Peter wrote concerning the church together in its gatherings is 5:1-5:

> Now as an elder myself and a witness of the sufferings of Christ, as well as one who shares in the glory to be revealed, I exhort the elders among you to tend the flock of God that is in your charge, exercising the oversight, not under compulsion but willingly, as God would have you do it—not for sordid gain but eagerly. Do not lord it over those in your charge, but be examples to the flock. And when the chief shepherd appears, you will win the crown of glory that never fades away. In the same way, you who are younger must accept the authority of the elders.

Here was a vision, not just of one leader, but of a group of leaders within the church. Just as James wrote of elders, so too did Peter. In James's context they were the ones to whom people would go for prayer. In Peter's context they were the leaders. As such, they were to be good examples of godly leadership, but they were also to be followed by the younger members of the church.

Tempting as it is to blend all of these columns together and give an outline of what biblical worship was in the first century, it is impossible to do. Some of these different elements have corresponding actions or portions of worship in other communities, but some do not.

ACTS 1	ACTS 2	ACTS 20	1 CORIN-THIANS	1 THESSALO-NIANS	HEBREWS	JAMES	PETER
					Temple language		
				Leaders		Elders	Elders
							Serving
		Sunday					
	Baptism						
			Hymns			Songs of praise	
Prayer	Prayer			Prayer		Prayer	
						Laying on of hands	
						Anointing with oil	
			Revelation	Prophecy			
			Tongues				
Scripture	Apostles' teaching						
Message	Apostles' teaching	Message	Lessons				Speaking
Response				Testing prophecy			
	Breaking bread	Breaking bread	Lord's Supper				
	Fellowship						
						Confession	
			Dinner		Meeting together		

It is true that not every author wrote everything that was happening in worship, yet that silence cannot be made into an argument for the missing elements if today's scholars are going to be honest with the historical knowledge presented in the Bible. Paul did not write of communal confession, and James did not write of the Lord's Supper. That does not mean that James's audience necessarily did not celebrate the Lord's Supper (the way Paul's communities did or otherwise), and it does not mean that Paul's communities necessarily did not practice confession (the way James's community did or otherwise), but neither does it mean that those respective communities did celebrate those two elements of worship. In the historical digging through these texts to see what the New Testament records of worship, the church of today is given glimpses into different communities. It is unwise to assume what happened in one also happened in all. Yet as noted before, these elements became the seeds of later worship throughout the church.

Early Church Worship

Outside of the Bible there are references to what constituted worship within the Christian community. Many of these are statements that only reference issues such as the sacraments. Some are more comprehensive in nature and give a more full and complete reference to worship. For the references that deal with the sacraments, those will be included in the relevant chapters later in the book. Once those are removed from the list of texts, there are a few writings from the earliest Christians that give the church a good look at worship. Part of the reason there are so few examples from the early years of the church is, not so much that it was assumed that all within the church would know what worship entailed, but that the worship service was kept secret from those outside of the church. Nonbelievers were not permitted to attend a Christian worship service. As well, those who were interested in becoming Christians, but not yet baptized, were not permitted to participate in all of the service. They only stayed for part of the service. Therefore, there are very few documents that explain what happened at a service, because Christians did not want the information to be known beyond their own group.

This was an age of persecution for Christians, and much of the persecution revolved around misperceptions of what happened within

Christian worship. There were charges of cannibalism and incest, as Christians reportedly ate flesh, drank blood, and had relationships with those they obviously called "brother" or "sister." It would have been a simple corrective to this misperception simply to open up Christian worship gatherings to outsiders and dispel any of these radically incorrect beliefs. Yet that is exactly what did not happen. Worship remained closed, and the accusations continued to fly. Practically speaking for the early church, this was a decision that may have reinforced some of the popular misconceptions about the faith. This is because they were not independently verifiable or deniable, and that gave Christianity an air of a mystery religion. Because mystery religions did have practices that were morally questionable to the greater Greco-Roman society, it was a short leap of logic to conclude the same about Christianity. While the belief systems and tenets of the faith of Christianity and any of the mystery cults were radically different, the fact that meetings were closed and certain similarities of sacramental actions were enough to see parallels. The main difference in the restriction in attendance at church worship services and mystery cults, though, was the ultimate reason behind the closed doors. In the mystery religions, which were primarily Gnostic in nature, the reason for exclusion of outsiders was to keep the secret knowledge as the treasure of only those who had been initiated into the mystery. For the Christian, however, outsiders were excluded because in their worship the holy and righteous God showed up. It was not exclusionary to preserve a special status or knowledge; it was exclusionary to protect the unbaptized. Secondarily it was to protect the worshiping community, although the courage Christians demonstrated in facing persecution shows that this was not the primary reason. When faced with the reality of being killed for the faith, many Christians chose to be killed. Practically speaking for today, it is also a bit frustrating when looking for primary source material on what early Christian worship was that the services were so closed.

Justin Martyr

The best witness of what the early Christians did in worship comes from Justin. He was born in Palestine, in the modern-day city of Nablus. He was not born to a Christian family, but he converted to the faith after a lengthy and exhaustive search for meaning through most of the belief systems of the day. He found in Christianity answers to the questions he had about the meaning of life. Eventually he made his way to Rome, and there he wrote two apologies defending the Christian faith, dedicated to the emperor Antonius Pius (father of Marcus Aurelius), around the year 150. This writing is important for not only what it recorded but for when it was written. Justin gave the emperor, and posterity, a general order of worship used by Christians in Rome only one hundred years after Paul wrote his epistles. Justin wrote:

> On the day named after the sun [Sunday], all who live in city or countryside assemble. The memoirs of the apostles [Gospels and perhaps Epistles] or the writings of the prophets are read for us as long as time allows. When the lector has finished, the president addresses us and exhorts us to imitate the splendid things we have heard. Then we all stand and pray. As we said earlier, when we have finished praying, bread, wine, and water are brought up. The president then prays and gives thanks according to his ability, and the people assent with an "Amen!" Next, the gifts over which the thanksgiving has been spoken are distributed, and everyone shares in them, while they are also sent via the deacons to the absent brethren.[2]

The passage by Justin is remarkably congruent with Acts 2. Equally remarkable, it could be a general outline of almost any worship service celebrated today that included the Lord's Supper. There is a gathering on Sunday, scripture reading, prayers, and Communion. In addition to these elements present in worship each week, Justin also detailed taking up a collection to be used to aid widows, orphans, the sick, those

---

2 Justin Martyr, *First Apology*, in *ANF*, 1.67.186.

in prison, strangers visiting from other congregations, and anyone else who had material need among the believers. This also mirrors many of the biblical elements found in worship, from Acts through the rest of the New Testament. It follows the basic pattern of calling out to God and receiving a response through the sacrament, as well. In fact, this outline that Justin recorded is so typical that it is the basis for worship from this point forward in history. From this worship service description, which is an embodiment of the basic grammar of worship, elements will be added or removed throughout times and places in history. Nevertheless, this is still the same essential worship service.

Early Liturgies

There are few other early sources that gave such a clear picture of worship as Justin. Some give much more detail, but only for one specific aspect of worship. Hippolytus gives extreme detail on ordination (specifically of a bishop), baptism and confirmation, as well as the Eucharist, and his work will be used later in corresponding chapters in this book for those elements of worship. Here, though, it can be noted that by the early third century (200s), Hippolytus of Rome composed his *Apostolic Tradition*. This work showed an order of worship that proceeded from ordination to prayers to the Lord's Supper. It also showed another order that moved from baptism to prayers to the Lord's Supper.

Contemporaneous with Hippolytus, and in Syria, the *Didascalia* also gives a picture of the life of the church. While this work did not list an order of worship itself, it does list the various people involved in worship and how they were to be arranged within the eastward-facing church building. These people according to their groups were bishops and priests, deacons, deaconesses, widows, and children. The reason for gathering together for worship, according to the *Didascalia*, was for teaching and celebrating the Eucharist.

Another lasting gift from the *Didascalia* is that it was used as the basis for an expanded collection approximately one hundred years later called the *Apostolic Constitutions* (ca. 300s). One section in this work expands on the different groups in the *Didascalia* and includes an order of worship detailing which group was responsible for which section. Typical of many works in this era, the Constitutions claimed the original apostles as their authors, and this section was attributed to Matthew.

> But be thou, O bishop, holy, unblameable, no striker, not soon angry, not cruel; but a builder up, a converter, apt to teach, forbearing of evil, of a gentle mind, meek, long-suffering, ready to exhort, ready to comfort, as a man of God.
>
> When thou callest an assembly of the church as one that is the commander of a great ship, appoint the assemblies to be made with all possible skill, charging the deacons as mariners to prepare places for the brethren as for passengers, with all due care and decency. And first, let the building be long, with its head to the east, with its vestries on both sides at the east end, and so it will be like a ship. In the middle let the bishop's throne be placed, and on each side of him let the presbytery sit down; and let the deacons stand near at hand, in close and small girt garments, for they are like the mariners and managers of the ship: with regard to these, let the laity sit on the other side, with all quietness and good order. And let the women sit by themselves, they also keeping silence.
>
> In the middle, let the reader stand upon some high place: let him read the books of Moses, of Joshua the son of Nun, of the Judges, and of the Kings and of the Chronicles, and those written after the return from the captivity; and besides these, the books of Job and of Solomon, and of the sixteen prophets. But when there have been two lessons severally read, let some other person sing the hymns of David, and let the people join at the conclusions of the verses. Afterwards let our Acts be read, and the Epistles of Paul our fellow-worker, which he sent to the churches under the conduct of the Holy Spirit; and afterwards let a deacon or presbyter read the Gospels, both those which Matthew and John have delivered to you, and those which the fellow-workers of Paul received and left to you, Luke and Mark.

And while the Gospel is read, let all the presbyters and deacons, and all the people, stand up in great silence; for it is written: "Be silent, and hear, O Israel." And again: "But do thou stand there, and hear." In the next place, let the presbyters one by one, not all together, exhort the people, and the bishop in the last place, as being the commander.

Let the porters stand at the entries of the men, and observe them. Let the deaconesses also stand at those of the women, like shipmen. For the same description and pattern was both in the tabernacle of the testimony and in the temple of God. But if any one be found sitting out of his place, let him be rebuked by the deacon, as a manager of the foreship [sic], and be removed into the place proper for him; for the church is not only like a ship, but also like a sheepfold. For as the shepherds place all the brute creatures distinctly, I mean goats and sheep, according to their kind and age, and still every one runs together, like to his like; so it is to be in the church. Let the young persons sit by themselves, if there be a place for them; if not, let them stand upright. But let those that are already stricken in years sit in order. For the children which stand, let their fathers and mothers take to them. Let the younger women also sit by themselves, if there be a place for them; but if there be not, let them stand behind the women. Let those women which are married, and have children, be placed by themselves; but let the virgins, and the widows, and the elder women, stand or sit before all the rest; and let the deacon be the disposer of the places, that every one of those that comes in may go to his proper place, and may not sit at the entrance.

In like manner, let the deacon oversee the people, that nobody may whisper, nor slumber, nor laugh, nor nod; for all ought in the church to stand wisely, and soberly, and attentively, having their attention fixed upon the word of the Lord.

After this, let all rise up with one consent, and looking towards the east, after the catechumens and penitents are gone out, pray to God eastward, who ascended up to the heaven of heavens to the east; remembering also the ancient situation of paradise in the east, from whence the first man, when he had yielded to the persuasion of the serpent, and disobeyed the command of God, was expelled.

> As to the deacons, after the prayer is over, let some of them attend upon the oblation of the Eucharist, ministering to the Lord's body with fear. Let others of them watch the multitude, and keep them silent. But let that deacon who is at the high priest's hand say to the people, "Let no one have any quarrel against another; let no one come in hypocrisy." Then let the men give the men, and the women give the women, the Lord's kiss. But let no one do it with deceit, as Judas betrayed the Lord with a kiss. After this let the deacon pray for the whole church, for the whole world, and the several parts of it, and the fruits of it; for the priests and the rulers, for the high priest and the king, and the peace of the universe.
>
> After this let the high priest pray for peace upon the people, and bless them, as Moses commanded the priests to bless the people, in these words: "The Lord bless thee, and keep thee: the Lord make His face to shine upon thee, and give thee peace." Let the bishop pray for the people and say: "Save Thy people, O Lord, and bless Thine inheritance, which Thou hast obtained with the precious blood of Thy Christ, and hast called a royal priesthood, and a holy nation."
>
> After this let the sacrifice follow, the people standing, and praying silently; and when the oblation has been made, let every rank by itself partake of the Lord's body and precious blood in order, and approach with reverence and holy fear, as to the body of their king. Let the women approach with their heads covered, as is becoming the order of women; but let the door be watched, lest any unbeliever, or one not yet initiated, come in.[3]

This is obviously a major portion of an ancient document, yet in it there is an order set forth that followed a very similar order to Justin Martyr in his *Apology*. These two works were composed almost two hundred years apart from each other, and in different regions of the Roman Empire, and yet the worship is similar enough that it would

---

3   *Apostolic Constitutions*, in *Ante-Nicene Fathers*, vol. 7, *Lactantius, Venatius, Asterius, Victorinus, Dionysius, Apostolic Teaching and Constitutions, 2 Clement, Early Liturgies*, ed. Alexander Roberts and James Donaldson (n.p.: Hendrickson, 1995), 421–22.

be familiar to people from each of the congregations represented by these traditions.

JUSTIN MARTYR	APOSTOLIC CONSTITUTIONS
People gathered together	People gathered together
Scripture readings	Reading of OT, Acts, Epistles by reader
Scripture readings	Reading of Gospel by deacon or presbyter
Message by president	Message(s) by presbyter/bishop
	Catechumens and penitents dismissed
Stand for prayer	Stand for prayer
Eucharist	Eucharist

What is even more interesting in the comparison of these two different orders of worship, separated by nearly two centuries and major geography, is that they came from two different liturgical families. Justin Martyr's worship became the foundation for the Western style of worship, and this description of worship in *Apostolic Constitutions* was from the Eastern style of worship. Yet even though they are from different liturgical families, there was such a similar order that it would seem, despite a lack of written evidence of early sources, the same basic order of worship was used throughout the church. The grammar for worship was set.

Modern Liturgies

To get from Justin Martyr and *Apostolic Constitutions* to today is a long route. There were many transformations to liturgies and worship services, both in the East and in the West. Items were added to services. Items were removed. Wholesale reconstruction and reordering of items happened. Multiple traditions merged and were transformed by one another. In the East, there were two main ways to worship: in the cathedral and in the monastery. Both of these ways were merged and,

THE ORDER OF WORSHIP

with the continued march of time, modified until around the 1600s. At the time of widespread use of the printing press, the Eastern service known as the Divine Liturgy solidified into the way it is celebrated today. Because of this fact, the Divine Liturgy is the exact same service all over the world, yet even in this rigid structure there are some accommodations for local traditions and special permission for slightly altering of the service. This means that in all practicality, the Divine Liturgy is always the same service, except for when it is not. The logic and the reasons why it may be changed are sometimes obvious, and sometimes, to use a pun, byzantine.

In the West, the liturgical development was a bit more involved, as several different, specific traditions were in use. There was the Ambrosian rite, which was centered in Milan. There was the Mozarabic rite, which was centered in Spain, and the Gallican rite, centered in France. There was the Gaelic rite, centered in Scotland and Ireland; the Sarum rite, centered in England; and an African rite, mostly used in North Africa. Over time each of these rites, along with others, came to be used less and less. Finally, after the Protestant Reformation, the Roman Catholic Church standardized the Roman rite, now known as the Tridentine Mass, after the Council of Trent. There are a variety of reasons why this decision was made, and the Tridentine rite had elements of many of the rites that came before it. This was one of the only rites allowed to be used for the Roman Catholic Church from 1570 to 1965 with the changes from Vatican II. The other ancient rites can be celebrated, but they require special permission from the local bishop. Usually, they are only celebrated within the communities that birthed them centuries ago. Otherwise, everyone uses the same Roman rite.

While the Eastern Orthodox service is still essentially the same as it was in the 1600s, the Roman Catholic service underwent serious reworking in the 1960s and 1970s, creating the *Novus Ordo*, the New Order. The service was greatly simplified, and Latin was virtually replaced overnight with the use of local, vernacular languages within the worship service. There were other, visual changes as well, mostly in the vestments worn by the clergy (see chapter 10). The Tridentine Mass is still used by the Roman Catholic Church, but now it is known as the "extraordinary" service, implying that the service that came out of the reforms of Vatican II are to be considered the "ordinary" service.

DIVINE LITURGY	TRIDENTINE MASS	NOVUS ORDO
Liturgy of Preparation	*Prayers at the Foot of the Altar*	
Liturgy of the Catechumens	*Liturgy of the Catechumens*	*Introductory Rites*
Litanies and Prayers	Prayers	Prayers
Little Entrance		
Trisagion Prayer		
		Liturgy of the Word
		1st Reading
Epistle	Epistle	Epistle
Gospel	Gospel	Gospel
Sermon (optional)	Sermon (optional)	Sermon
Litanies and Prayers for Living, Dead, Catechumens		
Liturgy of the Faithful	*Liturgy of the Faithful*	
Cherubic Hymn		
Great Entrance		
The Peace		
The Creed	The Creed	The Creed
		Litany
		Liturgy of the Eucharist
	Offering	Offering
	Washing of Hands	Washing of Hands
	Prayers	
Anaphora	Anaphora	Anaphora
Elevation	Elevation	Elevation
Lord's Prayer	Lord's Prayer	Lord's Prayer

THE ORDER OF WORSHIP

DIVINE LITURGY	TRIDENTINE MASS	NOVUS ORDO
		The Peace
Fracture	Fracture	Fracture
	The Peace	
Communion	Communion	Communion
		Concluding Rite
Litany	Antiphon	
Prayer	Prayer	Prayer
Dismissal	Dismissal	Dismissal
Post-Communion Prayers	The Last Gospel	

Although it may seem a bit cumbersome, each of these three services, the current Divine Liturgy of the Eastern Orthodox Church, the Tridentine Mass, and the Novus Ordo, all follow the same basic pattern and use the same grammar for worship. Some elements, such as the sign of peace, may be in different places, and some elements may be unique to one, like the entrances, but they still use the pattern of drawing near to God in litanies, prayers, and scripture, and then God drawing near to them in the sacrament of Holy Communion. There are many Protestant services that also fall into this basic pattern as well. The Service of Word and Table for The United Methodist church is extremely similar.

DIVINE LITURGY	TRIDENTINE MASS	NOVUS ORDO	WORD AND TABLE
Liturgy of Preparation	*Prayers at the Foot of the Altar*		
Liturgy of the Catechumens	*Liturgy of the Catechumens*	*Introductory Rites*	*Entrance*
Litanies and Prayers	Prayers	Prayers	Prayers
Little Entrance			
Trisagion Prayer			
		Liturgy of the Word	*Proclamation and Response*

93

DIVINE LITURGY	TRIDENTINE MASS	NOVUS ORDO	WORD AND TABLE
		1st Reading	1st Reading
Epistle	Epistle	Epistle	Epistle
Gospel	Gospel	Gospel	Gospel
Sermon (optional)	Sermon (optional)	Sermon	Sermon
Litanies and Prayers for Living, Dead, Catechumens			
Liturgy of the Faithful	*Liturgy of the Faithful*		
Cherubic Hymn			
Great Entrance			
The Peace			
The Creed	The Creed	The Creed	The Creed
		Litany	Prayers
			The Peace
			The Offering
		Liturgy of the Eucharist	*Thanksgiving and Communion*
	Offering	Offering	
	Washing of Hands	Washing of Hands	
	Prayers		
Anaphora	Anaphora	Anaphora	Anaphora
Elevation	Elevation	Elevation	
Lord's Prayer	Lord's Prayer	Lord's Prayer	Lord's Prayer
		The Peace	
Fracture	Fracture	Fracture	Fracture
	The Peace		
Communion	Communion	Communion	Communion
		Concluding Rite	*Sending Forth*
Litany	Antiphon		

DIVINE LITURGY	TRIDENTINE MASS	NOVUS ORDO	WORD AND TABLE
Prayer	Prayer	Prayer	
Dismissal	Dismissal	Dismissal	Dismissal
Post-Communion Prayers	The Last Gospel		

The only major difference between the United Methodist service and the Novus Ordo is the location of the peace and the offering in the service. It should be remembered, as well, that these are broad outlines of the services. There are several individual items that are contained within a heading. In addition, there are also portions of Psalms that are interspersed throughout the services along with hymns and other songs.

There are other Protestant services that do not have as many elements within them that could not make such a one-to-one correspondence with the Novus Ordo. Many of these services have been variously called different things at different times in history: low church, free church, revival, contemporary, praise. It is not wrong for these services to have fewer elements, but to allow for their people to experience the full scope of what worship can entail, they still need to follow the same basic grammar of worship. There needs to be an opportunity for worshipers to draw near to God, as well as an opportunity for God to draw near to the worshipers. Drawing near to God is usually an easier part of the service to provide for the people. This happens through prayers, songs, scripture readings, and sermons. The problem can arise when services rely solely on these elements for the entirety of the service. To have the same basic grammar, the service will necessarily need an opportunity for the people to experience God drawing near to them. Communion has been the traditional way this is experienced, yet it is not the only way. There can be opportunities for the people to experience God's presence through other means, such as focused prayer for conversion or sanctification. There can be experiences of the gifts of the Holy Spirit poured out upon the people in a Pentecostal service. This time could also be an intentional time of repentance for individuals and/or the community. There are many ways that this portion of the service could be made and implemented.

When John Wesley was forming the Methodist movement in the 1700s, he did not want the Methodists to separate from the Church of England. One of the ways he tried to keep the movement within the fold of the established church was to create the preaching service intentionally "defective." In a document known as "The Large Minutes," which was the original version of *The Book of Discipline*, Wesley said:

> Some may say, "Our own service is public worship." Yes; but not such as supersedes the church Service; it presupposes public prayer, like the sermons at the University. If it were designed to be instead of the church Service, it would be essentially defective; for it seldom has the four grand parts of public prayer, deprecation, petition, intercession, and thanksgiving.[4]

In the language of the eighteenth century, "public prayer" included the Eucharist. Wesley considered it defective precisely because it did not conclude with the Lord's Supper. The weekly preaching service consisted of hymns, prayer, and preaching from a text of scripture. There were all the elements of drawing near to God. Wesley wanted his people tied to the Church of England, and it was there they were supposed to experience God drawing near to them. This is not to say that God did not draw near to the people in either their class/band meetings or the love feast celebration, but in Wesley's mind it was more common for God to draw near to people through the ordinary means by which the presence of God was given—Holy Communion. It is a problem today when churches of whatever background use Wesley's "essentially defective" service as a model for worship today. Knowingly

---

4 Wesley, "Large Minutes" (1766), in *Works*, 10.326.

or unknowingly, services that eliminate the opportunity for God to respond take this defective service as a model.

As well, it must be remembered that the sermon is not and has never been a part of the service where God draws near to people. The sermon has always been on the side of the service of the people drawing near to God. The Bible, as Christians' sacred text, has already been given to humanity by God for the purpose of drawing close to God. The exposition of those texts in the form of sermons or homilies also is for the purpose of humanity drawing close to God. None of the most gifted preachers in church history have ever considered that their sermons were God descending to draw near to the people.

To be sure, there are many times, documented within recent and ancient history, where people have felt the power and presence of God through a sermon. People have experienced God speaking to them through a sermon. The entire camp meeting revival culture of the nineteenth and early twentieth centuries focused on preaching for that kind of a response and conversion. Yet even in those instances, the intended effect was for people to be drawn near to God so they could be transformed by the power and the presence of the Holy Spirit in their lives, all made accessible to them through a relationship with Jesus Christ. The sermon, as exposition on Scripture, was seen as a time when people could be brought nearer to God so they could experience grace and transformation in their lives at whatever stage they needed. These sermons were still intended to help the people draw near to God.

When preachers today, consciously or unconsciously, think of their sermons as the presence of God descending upon the people, it can set them up for burnout and disappointment in ministry. If someone is convinced that every message must bear the weight of bringing God to the people in a new and creative way so the congregation can respond to God's presence among them, it means that the preacher thinks of every message as divinely inspired and optimal for spiritual transformation. Obviously, there should be some level of inspiration in a sermon, but to view every sermon as the main point in a worship service in which God draws near to the people is a problem for one very simple reason: what happens when no one responds? There are two possible reasons when no one responds to God's presence drawing near to the people. First, it could be a problem with the preacher. Perhaps I am not as close to God as I thought. Perhaps I am not truly listening. Perhaps I am not as called to ministry as I thought, especially when I see the phenomenal responses to other preachers' sermons. Or second, it could be a problem with the congregation. Perhaps they are stiff-necked and hard-hearted. Perhaps they are bound by cultural forms of Christianity and are not open to the truth of the gospel. Perhaps I would have better success if I had a different congregation. Either of these responses, or a combination of the two, can lead to pastoral depression and frustration.

When the sermon is seen as one more opportunity for the people to draw near to God, then it is one tool among many that a congregation can use for that part of the service. This takes the burden off the preacher for every sermon to be, in some sense, a sacrament. To be sure, God's Spirit ought to be present within the construction and delivering of a sermon, but to the same degree as the Spirit is present in a worship song or an opening prayer. The church today would do well to allow the sermon to fit into the portion of the service it was designed to fit, that of helping the people draw near to God. This was how the earliest worship services understood the sermon, and it is how the classic, traditional services understood the sermon. Congregations today must also put the sermon on the correct side of the service.

5

THE CHURCH YEAR

Because the church is God's means by which all of creation is blessed and restored to what it was intended to be, the sanctifying process touches all aspects of human life. The church is in ministry to, with, and for people, sanctifying them as a holy nation and royal priesthood. The church sanctifies space and creates holy ground where people can step out of the ordinary, fallen creation and into a place that is set aside and dedicated to encountering God. The church also sanctifies time, creating a rhythm and order throughout life that enables people to experience, firsthand, the reality that God is a redeemer who has used historical instances and experiences to create the church and continues to speak and act in time to this day.

The Main Cycles

As a part of the process of sanctifying time, Christians over the centuries created two main cycles of celebration throughout the year. Both of these cycles follow the same basic pattern of *repentance—celebration—growth*. The reason for this cycle is because this is exactly the same cycle that an individual traverses when he or she moves closer to God in his or her own relationship. Whether it is initial conversion or victory over some entangling sin, the pattern for the individual is sincere repentance, celebration of conversion/victory, and further growth in grace and commitment to Christ. The church, in its wisdom, thought it would be beneficial for the cycle of life in the worshiping community to reflect this pattern and thereby reinforce and strengthen it in the lives of its people.

The first cycle is the *Advent—Christmas—Ordinary Time* cycle. The second cycle is the *Lent—Easter—Ordinary Time* cycle. It is not always readily apparent when looking at worship planners that these two cycles are identical. Often, particular Sundays are labeled as the *Xth Sunday after* whatever major celebration just occurred, which could be Christmas, Epiphany, Easter, or Pentecost. As well, some worship planners call the season after the Easter season Kingdomtide, which also obscures the identical nature of these cycles. Nevertheless, the reality is that these two cycles were intended to be identical in their flow in order to encourage the people in their experience and growth in grace.

Each of these cycles began as a preparation, not only celebrating a Christian holy day, but as a preparation for baptism. Much of the theology behind that issue will be covered in chapter 6, but for the purposes of this discussion it needs to be mentioned. At one point in the history of the church in its liturgical and pastoral development, baptism was only normally celebrated at Easter or Christmas/Epiphany. The time leading up to these holy days was intentionally carved out and set aside to prepare those who were going to be baptized for that sacrament. Over time, the emphasis in these periods of preparation became dual in nature. On the one hand, final preparations were made for baptism. On the other hand, emphasis was also placed on repentance and reconciliation of baptized members of the church to God and to one another.

It is an interesting theological and practical point that the cycles and rhythms of the Christian year were created and expanded out of a sense of pastoral care for Christians. They are essentially tools for the express purpose of discipleship. The celebration of a milestone in the life of Christ corresponds to milestones in the Christian life. These have times of preparation, study, and discipline before them. Then the celebration occurs. After the celebration, there is a normal, ordinary time of life and growth. These cycles take seriously the ebb and flow of everyday life and help connect Christians to the church and its theological realities through them. To participate in the Christian calendar and its cycles of fasting and feasting and growth is to help parishioners in their own discipleship process and gives the church a framework for that process so that it is not haphazard.

The period of preparation before Easter was designed to be forty days long in remembrance of Jesus's forty days in the wilderness before he began his public ministry. The English term *Lent* comes from a Germanic root for the spring season. In regions of the world that have a language descendent from Latin or with Greek influence the name is related to the number forty. How the forty days are counted is a bit of a mystery in the church. In the West, and those Christian traditions that are descended from the Roman way of calculating Lent, the season usually begins on Ash Wednesday and ends either just before the Last Supper is commemorated on the Thursday before Easter or the Saturday before Easter. This actually gives more than forty days, and the common way to reconcile this fact is by saying that Lent is forty days, not counting Sundays. The reason for this adjustment is that part of the discipline of preparation during Lent involves fasting, and the church frowned upon fasting on Sundays. This is because each Sunday is a mini-Easter, and thus a cause for celebration. In the East, and those Christian traditions that are affiliated with Orthodoxy, Lent begins on a Monday, and the Sundays during the season are counted. This still leaves extra days, and that is reconciled by the fact that Holy Week, the time from Palm Sunday to Easter, is seen as a time of intense fasting and preparation distinct from Lent itself.

Advent, which corresponds to Lent, is the season of preparation before Christmas. In the East, the Orthodox Church celebrates this season for forty days and sometimes refers to it as *Christmas Lent* or the *Nativity Fast*. The practice of observing a forty-day period of preparation before Christmas was also a part of the tradition in the West in many places (although to be fair, it was also celebrated as a period of three weeks, five weeks, and a few other configurations). Advent did not have the same overtly penitential emphasis that Lent did, and by around the year 1100, the season was officially fixed as a four-week time before Christmas.

The celebratory seasons of Easter and Christmas also share similarities while maintaining a uniqueness to themselves. The Easter Season lasts for fifty days and concludes with Pentecost. If fasting was an integral part of the Lenten season, this season has an equal emphasis on feasting. It is a celebration of the resurrection of Christ and his defeat of death and the powers of darkness. An unfortunate reality in many congregations today is that while there may be an emphasis on Lent and an attitude of repentance and spiritual preparation for Easter, the celebration of Easter is left to Easter Sunday alone. The party was meant to be extended for fifty days. Perhaps one of the ways to reacquaint the church with the celebratory nature of the good news without sacrificing the rhythm of the church year would be to reemphasize the fifty-day feast of Easter.

After Advent, the Christmas season lasts for twelve days. It ends with the celebration of Epiphany/Theophany. This is where the Twelve Days of Christmas, or Twelvetide, originated. This season has a bit of a convoluted history. Originally, the only day really celebrated in regard to the Incarnation is Epiphany/Theophany. The day, commemorated on January 6, has two distinct celebrations, each designated by a different name. It is called Epiphany, which means a realization, specifically when referring to the day as the day of the visitation of the Magi as recorded in Matthew's Gospel. This is the primary focus for most traditions in the West. In the East, the day focuses on the baptism of Jesus and is therefore referred to as Theophany, a revelation of God. No one is quite sure when the celebration of the actual birth of Christ began to be commemorated, but once it did, it was placed on December 25.

There are plenty of theories about how Christmas came to be celebrated on December 25. Some of those theories have a foundation in the idea that Christians took a date that was already being celebrated by Romans and "baptized" it to be a Christian celebration. This is what is at heart behind the idea that the celebration around the winter solstice, which was dedicated to *Sol Invictus*, the Unconquered Sun, was transferred to Jesus Christ. If this theory is true, it shows that Christians had no problem looking for the good in the cultures around them and then using those elements to point to the truth of the Christian message.

Another theory concerning the celebration of Christmas revolves around Jesus's death, and in Jewish, not pagan, roots. This theory states that Jesus was crucified on March 25. In some circles of Jewish mysticism of the day, God had perfect symmetry in the world. Therefore, they understood that holy and righteous people had the beginnings of life and the end of life on the same day. This means that if Jesus was crucified and died on March 25, this was also the day of his conception. Now March 25 is the feast of the Annunciation, the day the church celebrates Gabriel coming to Mary and announcing that she would conceive and bear the Son of God. Nine months after March 25 is December 25. This theory is bolstered by the fact that the Eastern portion of the church celebrated Christ's birth on January 6 rather than December 25, and they calculated Jesus's crucifixion and the Annunciation to April 6—exactly nine months before January 6.

Ways to Celebrate

There are several ways to acknowledge the liturgical cycles of the church in the life of a congregation. One of the first, and most obvious, is by how the worship space is decorated. Through *paraments*, pieces of cloth that are specific to the altar/Communion table and other furnishings in the sanctuary, banners, and other such variable items, the church can highlight the season of the Christian year. For exactly this purpose the church offers symbolic meanings that stand behind these colors that can be used during specific seasons. The most common color scheme in Western-tradition churches (Roman Catholic and Protestant) is purple-white-green. The time of preparation and repentance, Advent and Lent, are purple. The time of celebration, Christmas and Easter, are white. And the time of growth, Ordinary Time, is green. The reason for these choices is that the church equated purple with sorrow and a penitent spirit. Because Jesus had to die because of our sins, and because he was born so that he could die, both Lent and Advent were assigned the color purple. White was equated with purity, holiness, and celebration. Therefore, it was a fitting color to use to decorate for Easter and Christmas, when the church specifically focuses on the person of Jesus Christ, both his birth and resurrection. Green was equated with life and growth, and therefore it was viewed as a perfectly appropriate color for Ordinary Time, with its focus on spiritual growth and discipleship.

There are other colors that can be used throughout the year to highlight a specific aspect within the cycles. For instance, red is used on Pentecost to commemorate the Holy Spirit's descent as tongues of fire upon the church. Technically, that is the only day to use red; however, many traditions lengthen the time of red for one or more Sundays, especially since the season of Ordinary Time after Pentecost is so long. As well, many traditions will use red during ordination services or confirmation celebrations as a symbol of the presence of the Holy Spirit. Some traditions encourage the use of black at some point during the period of time between the Thursday before Easter through that Saturday. Black represents desolation, abandonment, and the spiritual forces of evil that were at work against Christ specifically during those three days. Also, pink (or rose) is used quite often during Advent to symbolize joy, since it was great joy that Christ came to creation.

The one place that the color pink makes its most prominent appearance is in the Advent wreath. This is a recent tradition in the life of the church (anything that is fewer than two hundred years old is relatively recent in the life of an entity that is two thousand years old) in which candles are lit for each of the Sundays of Advent. The Advent wreath itself may have symbolic roots in the menorah that is lit by Jewish believers in commemoration of Hanukkah, and it is popularly used as a way to help congregations (especially their children) count down to Christmas. Because purple is the color used during Advent, three of the four candles (the first two and the fourth) are purple. The third candle, however, is pink. The reason the third Sunday is different is that it is traditionally opened with the idea of rejoicing in the opening prayer. Because of this tradition, some people explain the purple of the first two candles as penitential, the third candle as joy, and the purple of the fourth candle to represent royalty, since Jesus is the Prince of Peace.

There is an even more recent tradition to use blue as the color for Advent rather than purple and pink. Blue is seen as a color of hope, which is one of the background meanings for the season of Advent, and using this color allows purple to be exclusively tied to the season of Lent. As well, it eliminates the confusing presence of pink in the midst of purple in the Advent celebration. The reason blue was chosen is that it is connected, legitimately or not, to the ancient Sarum rite from England. According to this tradition, the church in England before the liturgical monopoly of the Tridentine rite in the Roman Catholic Church, used blue during Advent. Because of this, churches that have a historical tie to England, namely Anglican and Methodist, have begun to use blue for Advent.

The colors used as symbols for the Christian year are not only used in decorating furniture or banners on the wall; they can also be used as a part of the clergy vestments. There are several different opinions on clerical dress for worship. If a pastor is going to wear a robe while presiding over worship services, it can range from a black robe and a stole that is in the color of the current Christian season to much more ornate types of clothing, such as surplices, chasubles, and other garments that are usually seen as "Catholic." Either way, the color of the current season is usually a prominent accent color in the vestments.

Something else that is akin to the Advent wreath, in that it is a way to signify a special season within the church year, is the Paschal candle. It is called paschal in reference to the Hebrew word for Passover, *pascha*. This is a very tall candle, usually three feet, and placed on an equally tall candlestand. The candle is a symbol of the pillar of fire that led the Israelites while they were being guided by God after the Exodus. As such, its purpose is to remind the congregation that Christ is their Passover and that the same Presence guides them to this day. As well, when a congregation uses a Paschal candle, it is usually lit at the beginning of the Easter service, while it is still dark, either late Saturday night or early Sunday morning. This is also symbolic of the light shining in the darkness and the darkness being unable to overcome it (see John 1:5). This candle is then lit at every worship service throughout the Easter season, which also reminds the congregation that Easter is actually fifty days long. The Paschal candle can also be used at any baptismal service beyond the Easter season as well. It is lit, and each person baptized, or the family of an infant baptized, is given a candle that is lit from the Paschal candle. In this way every baptism is connected with the symbolism of the Easter service and becomes a way to visually reinforce the reality that all baptisms are a participation in the death and resurrection of Christ.

Other Holy Days

Within the two main cycles of the Christian year, there are other holy days that can be commemorated. Some traditions celebrate more, some less, but they are days on the calendar nonetheless. There are reasons why Christians have set apart certain days throughout the year as holy. The first and main reason is that the Christian faith, like the Jewish faith, is one in which people celebrate God acting within history. What the church commemorates are events that truly happened and people who truly lived. It is a reminder that the faith is not an abstract concept or simply a set of beliefs but rather a relationship with a real God who really was and is involved in the world. Christmas, Easter, Pentecost, and the other holy days throughout the year commemorate real events in history. Jesus was truly born of a virgin. He truly rose from the dead. The Holy Spirit really was given to the church at Pentecost.

Another reason to set aside certain days as holy is that while there is no real distinction between sacred and secular (it is all God's time and therefore is all sacred), human beings have a serious problem living as if every moment is a holy and sacred moment to God. Just as the tithe was given to humanity to serve as a reminder that the whole was God's, holy days are in the calendar to remind the church that all time is holy. Celebrations and commemorations are observed as ways to remind Christians that God is still at work in the world today. Just as a wedding anniversary is one single day, it is also a reminder of the other 364 days of marriage. Holy days within the church calendar function the same way.

In light of that fact, there are other days that commemorate events in the life of Christ or the life and history of the church that are set apart as holy. Some of these are significant days in the life of Christ and are usually incorporated into the major cycles. Others are more about God's action in the world through people and events other than Jesus Christ, and they remind the church of the many different ways God was at work and is still at work in the world today. The days that are set apart in the Christian calendar are:

January 1	Circumcision of the Lord
January 6	Epiphany/Theophany
February 2	The presentation of the Lord
March 25	The Annunciation
Palm Sunday	Jesus's triumphal entry into Jerusalem
Maundy Thursday	Last Supper and foot washing
Good Friday	The Crucifixion
Easter Sunday	Resurrection of the Lord
Forty days after Easter	The Ascension
Pentecost	The outpouring of the Spirit/ the birthday of the church
Sunday after Pentecost	Trinity Sunday

August 6	Transfiguration
September 14	Holy Cross Day
November 1	All Saints' Day
November 2	All Souls' Day
Last Sunday before Advent	Christ the King
December 25	Christmas

Other days could be added to this list: for example, days that pertain to John the Baptist, his birth on June 24 or his beheading on August 29. There are days specific to Mary, most notably August 15, the date of her death (the Dormition). There are days dedicated to Christians throughout the ages that exemplified some aspect of the Christian life, such as Saint Patrick of Ireland (March 17), Saint Francis of Assisi (October 4), and Saint Nicholas (December 6). To these days could also be added May 24, Aldersgate Day (also the feast day of John and Charles Wesley in the Church of England) or October 31, Reformation Day (the feast day of Martin Luther in the Church of England). There are also local days that can be celebrated in the life of a congregation. The church can also set aside the anniversary of the congregation's founding, a homecoming celebration, and/or a major event in the life of the community, and so on. Because the church has a two-thousand-year history in general and individual denominations or congregations also have their own particular histories, the calendar of special days can be quite full. However, it is usually up to local leadership to decide how many days should be celebrated in a year.

The Lectionary

One of the keys to celebrating any festivals, feasts, or holy days in the life of the church is a *lectionary*. A lectionary is a series of readings from the Bible organized according to a regular schedule. Throughout the centuries there have been several different lectionaries in use.

Some have a fixed set of readings that were on a one-year cycle. Others were on a multiyear cycle. Some contained readings from every major section of the Bible, and some only focused on the Gospels. The most common lectionary used in the Western church today is the Revised Common Lectionary. This is a lectionary that was developed by representatives from most major denominations, including the Roman Catholic Church. Every Sunday of the year has at least four readings. The usual pattern for the readings is one from an Old Testament text, a psalm, one New Testament text, and one reading from a Gospel. If a particular congregation followed the entire lectionary throughout the entire three-year period, those parishioners would be exposed to the majority of the Bible.

There are many advantages for a congregation and pastor using the lectionary, especially if they are following the Christian year. First, the readings line up with the particular emphasis for that season of the year. The readings in Lent are more penitential in nature. The readings during the Easter season are more celebratory. The readings in Ordinary Time focus on the natural progression of growth in grace. The readings in Advent focus on the expectation for the arrival of Christ, both in a historical sense for his first arrival and prophetically, as all of creation awaits his second coming.

Second, following the lectionary forces the leadership of a particular congregation to move away from their favorite and familiar passages of scripture and helps them grow in their own spiritual development by interacting with portions of the Bible they would otherwise pass over. This enables pastors to avoid having a "canon within the canon," a certain favored set of readings that are the only ones they use in worship and preaching. Too many clergy eschew the lectionary under the mistaken impression that there is no way a set cycle of readings could accurately and pastorally address the immediate needs of the congregation. This actually misses the point of the lectionary. The church has had lectionaries from its earliest days, and some believe that Christianity inherited the practice from Judaism before it. The readings were prescribed for each service, but the exposition of that scripture reading, the sermon, was what varied according to the needs of the community. In this way the lectionary became a discipleship tool, not only for the congregation but for the preacher as well. The preacher was forced to study the biblical passage, proclaim the truth of that passage to the congregation, and give a practical reason why it matters in the life of the congregation at that point in time.

Finally, the use of the lectionary allows the leadership of a congregation more freedom to focus effort and energy on other pastoral and leadership issues. By not having to invent new series or by not having to struggle week to week with what scripture to proclaim, the pastor or pastors involved in the life of a particular congregation can devote more time to the people in their care. Not only does this free up valuable time in the life of a pastor, but it also can be a comfort as well. The pastor can be sure that the parishioners will hear from the full breadth of the biblical witness and be exposed to a holistic vision of the Christian life. This is because the lectionary, with its multiple readings on any given Sunday, gives the opportunity for congregations to hear more scripture. The burden for spiritual conviction or biblical discipleship is partially lifted from the pastor's shoulders, as the Bible itself is read to the people and the truths contained within it are communicated through the reading of it. In the Western world, where more Bibles are printed and fewer are being read on a regular basis, exposure to more scripture within the context of a worship service is an essential tool for discipleship.

The Revised Common Lectionary (RCL), the current version of the lectionary in use by many Protestant denominations (and with significant crossover with the current Roman Catholic lectionary, since that was the basis for the RCL), follows a three-year cycle in which the primary Gospel readings in Year A are from Matthew. Mark is the main Gospel for Year B. Luke is the primary Gospel for Year C. The Gospel of John is interspersed throughout all three years. Many times, the New Testament reading, either from one of the Epistles, Acts, Hebrews, or Revelation, will have a thematic connection with the Gospel reading. There are other times throughout the year, however, that these readings are not tied to the Gospel reading. Instead, they are continual readings through a particular book in the Bible. This is also true with the Old Testament readings. There are times when they are thematically connected, and there are times when it is simply reading straight through a book. Usually the readings are tied together thematically the closer the Sunday is to a major holy day, such as Easter or Christmas. By utilizing multiple readings on these days especially, a congregation can have their understanding of that particular holy day deepened and expanded.[1]

---

1   See Appendix D for the Revised Common Lectionary readings.

6

SACRAMENTS

When Jesus died on the cross, he was pierced by a spear. This was done, so the Gospel of John records in chapter 20, to see if he really was dead. Once his side was pierced, out flowed blood and water. Jesus was truly dead, and the stab in his side proved that. There are explanations as to why both blood and water poured from his side. One scientific explanation says that Jesus had been dead for so long on the cross that his blood and plasma had begun to separate. When he was pierced, they came out together, appearing like water along with the blood. Another explanation, though, has less to do with how this could have happened and more to do with what it means.

Taking our direction from Paul's writings among others, Jesus is the New Adam. He is the perfect human, a human fully and completely redeemed from the curse of the Fall in Genesis 3, because, not only was he without sin, but he conquered death as well. Jesus's bride is the church, all Christians who are in Christ. Adam fell into a deep sleep, and God took part of his side, a rib, to make Eve, his bride. Likewise, Jesus fell into the deep sleep of death, and God, through Jesus and the Holy Spirit, used his body to create the church, his bride. Water is used in the sacrament of baptism, signifying, among other things, that people are now a part of the church. The blood is found in the sacrament of Holy Communion, signifying, among other things, Christians' abiding presence and participation in the life of the church.

Some people see little importance in the sacraments beyond remembering what Jesus did for us almost two thousand years ago; yet for the church to be all it should be and could be, sacraments are essential because baptism and the Lord's Supper help create, maintain, and empower the church to be all Christ created it to be. Remember: Jesus created a church, a group of believers united together, not a bunch of individual believers that occasionally get together. Jesus said, "On this rock I will build my church and the gates of Hades will not overcome it" (Matthew 16:18). It is the church that is given the ability to storm the gates of Hades, and it is the church that has the power to overcome the strongholds of evil in the world.

Jesus created a church because we are mutually dependent upon one another. Each and every believer is given certain gifts—abilities, talents, resources, or callings—from God. No one believer is given all the gifts needed to fulfill the ministry that Jesus began in the Holy Land. The gifts are broken up and given over the entire body of believers; they are dispersed throughout the whole church. Thus, we have to work together and depend on one another to carry on the ministry of Jesus to proclaim the good news of the coming kingdom of God to the ends of the earth.

In the Life of the Church

The sacraments are an integral part of the life of the church, from being the entry point to the continued sustenance throughout our Christian lives. The very fact that the earliest Christians placed a strong emphasis on the sacraments in spite of persecution shows how important they understood these to be for them. Baptism was viewed as essential for membership in the church. Jesus commanded his followers to baptize as the church grew. Peter called on the crowd of hearers on Pentecost to repent and be baptized. If anyone could have laid a claim to not needing to be baptized, it would have been Paul with his Damascus road experience, yet even he was baptized by Ananias after being commissioned by Jesus Christ to be an apostle. And as early as the third century (200s), there was a debate as to whether or not infants ought to be baptized. The fact that this was debated shows how important the sacrament was for the early church. As well, extremely elaborate and beautiful ceremonies full of imagery and meaning arose to accompany the sacrament—ceremonies that show the high importance of the act in the life of the church. One of the earliest archaeological finds of Christianity is a baptistery from the church building in Dura-Europos dating from the early 200s, showing that baptism was of such importance that one of the sections of the home converted into a worship facility was an area to celebrate this sacrament.

Likewise, the Lord's Supper was extremely important in the life of the church. There are numerous places in the New Testament where the sacrament is celebrated or discussed. There are numerous texts outside of the New Testament that have Communion rituals recorded, or at least the general flow of the service explained. From the historical documents we have, it is clear that the early church celebrated the Lord's Supper weekly and it was seen as an integral part of the worship service—so much so that without the sacrament, it really was not a church service. On top of this, there are several accounts of persecution during the first three hundred years of the church in which one of the charges was that the Christians were cannibals, eating flesh and drinking blood. Despite these charges, the Christians did not give up celebrating Holy Communion at all. The sacrament was of such importance to them that they endured the misunderstood charges against them and continued to celebrate it weekly. Because the sacraments were, and are, essential to the life of the church, John Wesley drew on his Anglican theology and tradition by writing that the sacraments were *means of grace*, "ordinary channels" by which God gives grace to humanity. Yet there is a large question that this understanding elicits: What is grace?

This is a question many people do not usually ask, but how we, as representatives of the church, answer it will largely form how we relate to God, the church, and the world-at-large around us. If "by grace you have been saved through faith" (Ephesians 2:8), then we ought to know what we mean when we use the word *grace*. Some people define grace as unmerited favor. It is certainly true that anything we receive from God is unmerited, because we could never live up to the standard of holiness that God has, but this cannot be an adequate definition of grace. Unmerited favor is really mercy born out of compassion, not grace. They are interrelated but not the same.

Some people talk about grace as if it is some kind of divine pixie dust that God sprinkles on us. In this understanding, we receive this gift of grace like a present, a package, or perhaps a coat. We are covered with grace or it is poured over us, and we try to receive more of this grace so we can be "filled up" or "grace-filled." An understanding of grace like this leads people to see the sacraments or worship or any religious activity in life as a way of earning more grace to go in the box, wrap around us, or fill us up. The more grace we earn, the better off we will be in life. Grace begins to be thought of as a commodity that is gained or lost depending on one's life, attitudes, and behaviors.

Some people explain grace as *God's love*. This is a fine statement, but it can be a little misleading, because this understanding of grace only works in cultures that are stable and when Christians are secure and well-off. This definition of grace fails in the face of faithful Christians who lose everything because they have been persecuted or had to watch their loved ones tortured and killed before their eyes for the faith. Saying that grace is God's love is also a bit of a circular statement since God is love, but this does get close to the heart of what grace is.

Grace woos us toward God. It enables us to respond to God. Grace gives us the power to overcome sin in our lives and the world in general. It deepens our relationship with God and makes us more completely reflect the image of God in which we were created. Having said all that, it would not be a great leap to say that grace is the name we give to the experience of the presence of God in our lives. This is because the Holy Spirit could be substituted in the above statements everywhere the word grace appears and it would still make sense. It is the Holy Spirit, active in the world, who woos us toward God. The word *grace* then becomes a shorthand term for the power and presence of God in our lives in the person of the Holy Spirit. This even makes sense of Ephesians 2:8, quoted above. We are saved by God's power and presence in our lives through faith.

If we respond favorably to the prompting and wooing of God through the Holy Spirit (grace), we come to feel the presence of the Holy Spirit even more. The more we respond to grace/the presence of the Holy Spirit, the more we experience the presence of God. It is not that we receive more of some substance that will help us be "grace-filled"; rather, we recognize the leading of God more readily and more completely in our lives. Essentially, we get ourselves out of the way of God working in our lives. The more we, in Jesus's words, deny ourselves (see Matthew 16:24), the more we are "filled." Soon, we come to the point of believing that Jesus is God incarnate and accept that he is the only way to not only feel promptings from the Holy Spirit, but to actually be able to converse with God through the Holy Spirit and call on his power to overcome sin and temptation in our lives.

So, grace is not simply unmerited favor. Nor is grace some kind of divine stuff that we can accumulate in our lives. Nor is grace completely explained by God's love. Grace is God. It is God's presence in our lives to empower us to live, love, and overcome in a manner that is pleasing to God. It is the active working of God within us as we allow the Holy Spirit to transform us more and more into the image and likeness of Jesus Christ. As we listen to that leading in our lives, and as we accept what God is trying to do in us to make us more Christlike, then we will be able to grow even more in that direction. The more we move toward God through grace-filled promptings in our lives, the more we recognize God's presence and the easier it becomes to affirm and accept God's presence and leading, and the further we "grow in grace" (see 2 Peter 3:18). If grace is God's presence in our lives, then this leads to another question.

The question, though, is how God actually uses physical objects—bread, fluid from a grape, water—to convey grace to us. If grace is

God's presence in our lives, why would we need to have anything like sacraments? After all, does God not come to us in prayer and worship and reading scripture or even walking in the woods and enjoying creation? Yes, God can and does come to us in these ways, and a whole host of others as well. However, we ought not to overlook one very important fact: God created physical things. Not only did God create physical things; God created them "very good" (Genesis 1:31). The created universe is not how God originally made it, but God is in the process of redeeming all of creation, so that it will be very good once again.

In light of this it is no wonder God should use physical things to work in this world. After all, God took on a physical form to enable our salvation and begin the process of restoration. If God were not concerned with matter and the physical universe, Jesus Christ would not have become incarnate and taken on our physical nature. This means that God will use whatever is needed to convey grace to humanity and work for our salvation.

The classic definition of a sacrament is that it is an outward and visible sign of inward and spiritual divine grace; a sacrament is an object or act that stands in the place of what is signified. A summary way to phrase it is that it is an outward sign of an inward grace. Going through the act of baptism shows a commitment to God and that God is present and at work in the life of the one being baptized. Participating in the Lord's Supper shows a reception of the life and work of Christ and that Christ is present in the communicant's life. As physical beings, God gave us physical things and contract acts—sacraments—to help us understand with our whole being the truth of the gospel. In addition, these physical actions allow us to worship God with all of our being, not just our intellect or our spirits, but our bodies with all of our senses. Because God uses the physicality of the sacraments to convey grace to us, it allows our entire being to be involved in the adoration of our Lord and God and Savior Jesus Christ, and it reminds us that our redemption is not just spiritual but physical as well.

SACRAMENTS

The word *sacrament* comes from the Latin *sacramentum*, which was the oath of allegiance a soldier took when he joined the military. This connotation is present in baptism and the Lord's Supper, because they are signs of our allegiance to Christ as our Lord. The Greek term for a sacrament is the word *mysterion*, or *mystery*. This connotation reminds us that it truly is a mystery how God connects to us through the physical elements of bread and cup and water (Communion and baptism) to his body—his blood and water that flowed down from the cross—God's mighty salvific act through Jesus's great sacrifice. This symbolism is important to keep in mind as we look at the differing interpretations and debates surrounding these two rites of Christian worship. It is ultimately a mystery. We can have ideas, theories, traditions, and can support them with biblical passages. Ultimately, however, God alone knows how these work in people's lives. God alone knows why it is possible to use physical objects to convey grace to us.

THE SACRAMENT OF BAPTISM

Practical Issues

For the sacrament of baptism there are three practical debates and issues: Who can receive the sacrament? Is the sacrament repeatable? and What is the acceptable mode of baptism? Each of these questions has people who believe very strongly that they have the correct answers, and some of those who are convinced they are correct have opposite understandings of the issues. Entire denominations stay separated over these issues, and there are even some well-meaning Christians who would question the validity of another Christian's salvation experience if that person's baptism did not agree with their understanding and belief.

Who Can Receive Baptism?

This question speaks to the core issue of different understandings of baptism. There are those congregations, denominations, and traditions that strongly adhere to the understanding that only believers ought to be baptized. In other words, only those individuals who can make a conscious choice to accept the offer of salvation made through the life, death, and resurrection of Jesus Christ ought to be baptized. On the other side of the issue are those congregations, denominations, and traditions that strongly adhere to the understanding that infants and children of believers ought to be baptized. In other words, the sacrament of baptism is bigger than an individual accepting a saving faith in Christ.

The biblical witness concerning baptism is found in short snippets of text throughout the entire New Testament.

JOHN THE BAPTIST'S MINISTRY	BELIEVERS BEING BAPTIZED
Matthew 3:1-12; 21:25	Acts 8:12-13, 36; 9:18
Mark 1:2-8; 11:30	**HOUSEHOLDS BEING BAPTIZED**
Luke 3:1-18; 7:29-30; 20:4	Acts 10:47; 16:15, 33; 18:8
John 1:19-34; 3:22-26	1 Corinthians 1:16
Acts 10:37; 13:24	
JESUS'S BAPTISM	**BAPTIZED INTO JESUS'S DEATH**
Matthew 3:13-17	Romans 6:4
Mark 1:9-11	Galatians 3:27
Luke 3:21-22	Colossians 2:12
JESUS AND HIS DISCIPLES' BAPTISMAL MINISTRY	**BAPTISM AS UNITY**
	1 Corinthians 12:13
John 3:22-26; 4:1-2	Ephesians 4:5
Acts 1:22	**EXPLAINED WITH OLD TESTAMENT IMAGERY**
JESUS'S SUFFERING AS BAPTISM	1 Corinthians 10:2
Mark 10:38-39	Colossians 2:11-12
Luke 12:50	1 Peter 3:21
THE DIFFERENCE BETWEEN JESUS'S AND JOHN'S BAPTISMS	**BAPTISMAL CONTROVERSY**
Acts 1:5; 11:16; 18:25-26; 19:2-7	1 Corinthians 1:13-17; 15:29
AS A KEY COMPONENT OF SALVATION	**AN ELEMENTARY ISSUE OF THE FAITH**
Matthew 28:18-20	Hebrews 6:2
Mark 16:16	
Acts 2:38, 41	

These passages on baptism give a lot of information on the sacrament, from theology to example, but they do not shed much light on the issue of who ought to receive it. There are the examples of John the Baptist, who baptized people as they responded to the message he proclaimed about the need for forgiveness of sins, yet it is obvious from Scripture that Christian baptism is distinct from the ministry of John and his baptism. There are the admonitions of Peter and other apostles for people to respond to their proclamation of the good news in Jesus Christ by being baptized, yet there are also instances where entire households are baptized. Both practices use scripture to support their respective understandings, so it becomes a question of interpretation of scripture as to which position to hold.

The only way to begin to understand who ought to be baptized is to look beyond the New Testament texts to the practice of the early church. Here, unfortunately, there is no text that simply states, "Baptize the children of Christians" or "Only baptize converts." Rather, the earliest writing that deals with the question of whether or not children ought to be baptized comes from Tertullian of Carthage, who lived from AD 145 to 220. This puts Tertullian in the third generation of Christians. He would have been taught by those who were taught by the original disciples and apostles of Jesus (or the fourth generation at the latest). Tertullian himself was a convert to the faith at a later stage of his life and wrote extensively, both in defense of the faith and also to build up the life and purity of the church.[1]

In one of his earlier works, Tertullian wrote a treatise titled *On Baptism*. In this work he discussed several important aspects of the sacrament. These range from why water is used to Old Testament imagery. He answered many objections concerning baptism and showed why it is extremely important in the life of the church. Near the end of the treatise, Tertullian raised an objection to the baptism of young children (or infants). He did not think it was wise to baptize children, who were still innocent in life, nor did he think it was appropriate to entrust "divine matters" to ones who could not be entrusted with earthly matters because they were too young to be of legal age for inheritance or civic duties.

At first glance this would seem to confirm that the early church only baptized converts, and the practice of infant baptism was a later

---

[1] Toward the end of his life, Tertullian began to associate with the Montanist movement. This was an early heretical sect that thought a new outpouring of the Spirit signaled the imminent end of time. It was apocalyptic, charismatic, and extremely puritanical in what it believed constituted the holy Christian life. Nevertheless, Tertullian was a brilliant theologian and had a long and faith-filled life.

development. However, what is most interesting about this objection is the fact that Tertullian had to make an objection at all. In other words, infants were being baptized in the late 100s, and Tertullian disagreed with the practice. Just as warning labels on objects today mean that someone somewhere actually did what the rest of society is now warned not to do, so too objections to practices in church history mean that someone somewhere was doing exactly that which was being written against. For a treatise that was intended for widespread reading and distribution to take on an issue, that also meant that the issue was most likely widespread. This means that the practice of baptizing infants was widespread enough at the close of the second century that Tertullian thought it best to include his opinion, contrary to the prevailing attitude within the church, in a treatise that would be widely read. There is really only one explanation for how the practice could have been so widespread throughout so many of the congregations at such an early date in the life of the church—infant baptism was practiced from the beginning and was taught to many of the new faith communities by the original missionary apostles. Tertullian's case for objecting to the practice fed into a theological tradition known mainly in North Africa (where Carthage was located, in modern-day Libya) where people would postpone baptism until as close to the point of death as possible. This was because they read passages such as Hebrews 10:26-31 to mean that willfully committed sins after baptism lead to condemnation, with no opportunity for repentance.

If the practice of infant baptism was from the earliest days of the church, where is it in the New Testament? The closest we have to a written account is the description of the baptism of entire households in Acts and in 1 Corinthians. Here we have the households of Cornelius, Lydia, the Philippian jailer, Crispus, and Stephanas being baptized. Households included all of the men, women, children, and servants/slaves who were dependent upon the head of the house. It may even have included the married children (and their children) if they had not yet struck out from the dependency of the head of the household. When we are told entire households were baptized, this would be a significant number of people, including children.

But why would children receive baptism if the main injunctions in scripture are to *repent and be baptized*? Infants cannot repent. This is true, but it is not the only image of baptism in the New Testament. Colossians 2:11-12 states:

> In him also you were circumcised with a spiritual circumcision, by putting off the body of the flesh in the circumcision of Christ; when you were buried with him in baptism, you were also raised with him through faith in the power of God, who raised him from the dead.

This image equates baptism to circumcision. This is an important point. Jewish male children were circumcised on the eighth day after birth. This was not dependent upon the faith of those children. It was because they were born into the covenant people of God, Israel. It is logical to see how the earliest Christians, who were all Jewish or at least God-fearing Gentiles—Gentiles who believed that the God of Abraham, Isaac, and Jacob was the one true God but did not officially convert to Judaism—would understand there to be another symbol of covenant for their children. In this case, the covenant would be open not just to males, but females as well. This reminds Christians that in Christ there is neither male nor female (Galatians 3:28).

Does this negate the response of faith in the Christian life if infants can be baptized and included in the people of God? Not at all. Continuing with the Old Testament imagery being applied to baptism in the New Testament, Paul answered this exact issue. In 1 Corinthians 10:2-5, Paul wrote:

> And all were baptized into Moses in the cloud and in the sea, and all ate the same spiritual food, and all drank the same spiritual drink. For they drank from the spiritual rock that followed them, and the rock was Christ. Nevertheless, God was

not pleased with most of them, and they were struck down in the wilderness.

Here is the response to the question. Paul went so far as to say that passing through the Red Sea was baptism and not everyone who passed through those waters of deliverance availed themselves of the new life that was offered to them. Infants may be included in the covenant, but it is up to them as individuals whether or not they are faithful to that covenant.

This, then, brings up the issue of confirmation. Confirmation is a ceremony that has an interesting existence. Originally, in the history of the church, the three events of baptism with water, anointing with oil, and the Eucharist were all administered to a new convert one right after another. This means that one was baptized for the forgiveness of sins and into Christ's death and resurrection; then that one was anointed with oil for the reception of the Holy Spirit. Immediately after that event, the newly baptized and anointed one would receive the Lord's Supper for the first time. Even infants were brought into the faith in this manner, and that is the way the Eastern Orthodox church still does it today.

In the West, however, these three events quickly became separated from one another for a variety of reasons. One of the main reasons was that in the Western tradition only a bishop could administer the anointing with oil. As bishops were not in every town, and sometimes they were quite a distance away, this part of the initiation service was detached from baptism, which any priest could administer. The result is that in the Roman Catholic Church today, an infant is baptized, the child receives her or his First Communion around seven or eight years old, and then that child is anointed with oil at around twelve years old. That anointing is now *confirmation*. The sacrament (and it is a sacrament for the Roman Catholics) is now the opportunity for the child to make a profession of faith for himself or herself, *confirming* the profession of faith the parents made during the baptism years earlier on his or her behalf. This practice was carried over, to a large extent, into those Protestant denominations that retained infant baptism after the Reformation. Most eliminated the delay between baptism and the Lord's Supper so that as soon as a child could receive the elements, she or he was welcome to the Eucharist, but confirmation was still administered later in childhood.

Confirmation is meant to be the opportunity to wed together the serious commitment to the covenantal nature of baptism and the historical reality of infant baptism with the need for those members of churches to have a living faith for themselves. Within the Wesleyan/Methodist tradition, confirmation serves exactly this function. While confirmation is not seen as a sacrament in this tradition, and thus it is not absolutely necessary in the life of a believer,[2] it is an opportunity for all members of a congregation to have the privilege and experience of bearing witness to their faith. It is important to understand that confirmation does not add something that was missing from an infant's baptism; rather, it is a celebration of faith and a reminder to all that those who have a living faith in the triune God are filled with the Holy Spirit.

Is Baptism Repeatable?

This is a question that gets asked, especially if someone grew up in a Christian tradition where she was baptized as an infant but now affiliates with a tradition that does not believe in infant baptism. Can she be rebaptized? Of course, on one level this is a silly question. Yes, someone can be baptized more than once. The real question is: Should she be rebaptized?

There are many reasons someone might want to be rebaptized.

---

2 It is true that John Wesley did not include a service for confirmation in his service book for the new Methodist Episcopal Church in America in 1784. Some scholars have seen this omission as Wesley's subtle rejection of the baptism of infants. More likely, Wesley did not want anyone to think that he, Thomas Coke, or Francis Asbury were bishops (as he called them, superintendents). In the Anglican tradition, like the Roman Catholic tradition, a bishop is the only one allowed to administer the rite of confirmation, so that is why the rite was not included.

Perhaps this individual left the church and led a life that is the antithesis of a Christian life. Now this person has reconnected with God and wants to declare publicly his or her newfound faith. Perhaps a person has grown up within the church and, upon seeing older people converting and being baptized, wants to experience this sacrament in a way that he or she can remember. Perhaps a person was baptized as a preteen when all of her friends were baptized, without actually having any faith concerning the sacrament or Jesus Christ, but now that she truly has a faith in Jesus, she wants to be baptized again.

If baptism is seen primarily as covenant, as in the case of infant baptism, then the short answer to the question of whether or not baptism is repeatable is *no*. That a person is not faithful to the covenant with God into which he entered (or into which he was entered by his parents) does not mean that God is unfaithful to that covenant. When the person repents and turns to Christ, he will now be fulfilling his end of the covenant. There is no need to reinstitute it because one of the parties to the covenant, God, has always fulfilled his part of it.

In addition to this covenantal understanding of baptism, there is also another consideration for why it would not be theologically appropriate to rebaptize someone. Just because a person did not understand what was happening in the sacrament does not mean it needs to be repeated at a later date when he has a better understanding. Christianity is not a religion of knowledge and intellect. We cannot explain many key facets of the faith, such as the Trinity (God is three persons but one God); the Incarnation (Jesus Christ is fully God and fully human); or redemption (one man's sacrifice atones for all others). They are a mystery. Our level of comprehension of the faith is not a determining factor in our relationship with Jesus Christ. If that were true, all faithful Christians would have to get at least a seminary-level education in Christianity before we could say they were faith-filled, and even then, it would be debatable as to whether or not they had enough comprehension since an incomprehensible God is the object of our faith.

Instead, we can affirm that people may believe in God and be in Christ without completely understanding what that means. Very few people, even those with seminary-level educations, can explain how God the Spirit could dwell inside of a human being. This means that the reality for someone that "I didn't understand what was happening when I got baptized," does not mean that the baptism is invalid or that it needs to happen again. Think of marriage, or any other relationship. No one completely understands the depth of a relationship at the beginning of it. Most people on their wedding day have no clue how deep and transformative that relationship is going to be over the next few decades. Just so with baptism; that is the entry point into the relationship with God from a sacramental point of view. The sum total of the relationship would not yet be known, if it ever could be. This is true because, again, the God with whom we enter into this relationship is infinite. This means that there is never going to be a point in the relationship when we can finally "arrive" at fully knowing God.

Practically speaking, then, this means that when someone wishes to be rebaptized, it would be better classified as renewing one's baptism. The experience is still just as real for the person. The public display of commitment to Christ is affirmed. The desire to start in a definitive way the Christian life once again is fulfilled. And in addition to these concerns, by affirming that this is a renewal of an earlier baptism, it reminds all involved that God's grace is ever present in our lives. It can also serve as a teaching moment to proclaim to all who can hear that God's back is never turned on us, even if we had turned our backs on God. It is an opportunity to show the people present a real-life example of the parable of the prodigal in Luke 15:11-32!

How Do We Baptize?

A Baptist preacher and a Methodist preacher were discussing baptism:

> **Baptist**: I don't know why you Methodists insist on saying that sprinkling a little bit of water on someone's head

is a valid baptism. The plain meaning of scripture is clear on this—baptism is going all the way under the water with your whole body.

Methodist: Let me get this straight. You're saying if I go into the water up to my waist, it isn't a valid baptism?

Baptist: That's exactly what I am saying. You have to go all the way under.

Methodist: So if I go up to my armpits it doesn't count?

Baptist: No! Like I said, you have to go all the way under the water to be baptized.

Methodist: So if I go up to my chin it doesn't count?

Baptist: What part of this are you not understanding? You have to go all the way under the water and come up for a valid baptism.

Methodist: So if I go up to my eyebrows—

Baptist: No! That is not a valid baptism! The water has to be *over* your head.

Methodist: That's what I've been trying to tell you all along. It's the little bit of water on the top of the head that makes all the difference in the world!

This joke is all too real in many communities. There are serious debates concerning not just who to baptize or whether or not to re-baptize, but even how to baptize. Some congregations will not even consider a baptism valid unless it was a full-immersion baptism in their particular church building. The problem arises because there are three different ways congregations baptize. There is full-immersion baptism, where the one being baptized goes completely under the water and then comes back up out of the water. There is the practice of pouring water over the head. There is also the practice of sprinkling water on the forehead or crown of the one being baptized. People can get very upset over the question of how much water should be used in baptism.

Biblically, there are no instructions for how to baptize, only that Christians are to baptize. For the earliest directions on how to baptize, we have to look at that wonderful ancient text, the Didache, written sometime between AD 50 and 150. This text is made up of two sections. First, there is a discourse on the "Way of Life" and the "Way of Death." These two concepts are described with guidelines on what a faithful Christian life looks like when lived out. After this section, there is a list of instructions on how to administer the sacraments and how to lead in a congregation. In chapter 7, entitled "Concerning Baptism," the author wrote:

> And concerning baptism, baptize this way: Having first said all these things, baptize into the name of the Father, and of the Son, and of the Holy Spirit, in living [running] water. But if you have no living water, baptize into other water; and if you cannot do so in cold water, do so in warm. But if you have neither, pour out water three times upon the head into the name of Father and Son and Holy Spirit. But before the baptism let the baptizer fast, and the baptized, and whoever else can; but you shall order the baptized to fast one or two days before.[3]

Here we have the first instance of a description of how baptism is performed and celebrated in the life of the church. The ideal mode of baptism was immersion (and heavily implied in the original language a three-fold immersion) in cold, running water. This, evidently, was the way in which the community that was responsible for compiling the Didache were taught to baptize in the beginning of their churches. In this case, the Baptist in the above joke would have been correct, at least if he practiced triple immersion!

Yet notice that in the Didache there was also an acknowledgment

---

3   *Didache*, in *ANF*, 7.379.7.

that the ideal could not always be had when baptizing people. Sometimes the water may not be cold. Sometimes it may not be running, but instead it is a lake or a bath. Sometimes there may not even be enough water to fully immerse the one being baptized. In instances like this, water is to be poured over the top of the head, and this is seen as a valid baptism. The interesting point to this work is that there is a real attempt to take the sacramentally theological truth and understand it in the everyday realities of life. Some communities in which the church spread did not have rivers or streams, but were deserts. Some communities were more hostile to Christianity than others, and required baptisms behind closed doors. The mode did not negate the efficacy of the sacrament. In the church building uncovered in Dura-Europos, the baptistery was only large enough for someone to stand in, while water was poured over his or her head.

Today, we have three main modes of baptism: immersion, pouring, and sprinkling. Each one has a theological truth tied to it with a symbolic meaning attached. Immersion baptism reminds us that we die with Christ and rise again to new life in him. Just as a dead body is put under the earth, so too is the one to be baptized put under the water. When the baptized Christian rises out of the water, it is as if this person has been resurrected to new life and is now a "new creation" in Christ. When water is poured out over the head of the one being baptized, it reminds us that in becoming Christian the Holy Spirit is poured out over us. Just as the Holy Spirit was poured out on the first Pentecost, and Peter reminded his hearers on that day that God had promised to pour out his Holy Spirit on all flesh, so too is the one baptized the recipient of that promise of the presence of the living God in his or her life. When water is sprinkled over the forehead or crown of the one being baptized, it reminds us that when we become Christians we are anointed to be a royal priesthood. Just as priests and kings were anointed with oil in the Old Testament to set them apart for a special calling in life, so too we are a kingdom of priests and a royal nation, anointed by God and set apart for a special life and mission in the world (1 Peter 2:9).

Theological Issues

The main theological issue concerning baptism concerns what happens in baptism. Does the sacramental act of baptism do something to the one being baptized? In other words, is there such as thing as baptismal regeneration? How one approaches this single issue will determine, to a large extent, how the practical issues and debates just described are resolved. If a person is regenerated in the act of baptism, if the act of baptism is intrinsically linked to salvation, the administration of this sacrament will take on a different meaning than if the converse were true. Different denominations take different approaches to this issue, and those differing opinions then result in divisions between groups that believe in "one Lord, one faith, one baptism" (Ephesians 4:5).

Historically, the dominant view in the earliest days of the church through the first several centuries was that baptismal regeneration was true. In the sacramental act of experiencing baptism, the one being baptized was truly born "of water and the Spirit," and this was a necessary part of salvation (see John 3:5). The only exception to this rule was if a catechumen, one who was learning the faith but not yet Christian, was martyred for the faith. In that case, it was said that the person was baptized in his or her own blood, and thus was given a Christian funeral and burial. Yet even in these cases baptism was still seen as so essential that the martyrdom itself is still called *baptism*. As well, many people took passages in Hebrews and 1 John extremely seriously. These biblical texts imply that Christians do not sin; and if they do fall away from the faith, there will be no opportunity for restoration or salvation after that sin, consequently baptism was often postponed even for believers until the end of life. In that way there would be less opportunity to sin after baptism. This is the most likely reason that Constantine postponed his own baptism until his deathbed. He lived under the assumption that sin subsequent to baptism meant separation from Christ and no possibility of redemption. This was one particular tradition within the church that eventually fell out of belief and practice.

As the church moved away from the idea that sin after baptism was condemnatory, fewer and fewer people postponed their baptisms. This, coupled with Augustinian theology about original sin and all of humanity's participation in the guilt of it (including infants), the necessity of baptism persisted. Only now baptism was essential for all people from birth, as all were guilty under Adam's sin. Baptismal regeneration undid the guilt of that sin, and the baptized, even if an infant, was now a new creation and thus born again. This remained the dominant view of baptism for centuries and is still the understanding of baptism in Roman Catholic and Eastern Orthodox churches to this day (as well as some Protestant denominations).

The theology of baptismal regeneration was questioned most publicly during the Reformation. Because of the emphasis on faith for salvation rather than any action, the link between salvation and baptism was broken. This, coupled with the distinction between being born into a nationality but having to choose to be in the kingdom of God, led to a further eroding of the necessity of baptism within segments of the church. The irony today is that even for denominations that do not practice believers-only baptism, there is still a question about the necessity of baptism. If it is belief that saves a person, the actual act of baptism becomes secondary or even superfluous. This is not to say that there is not logical sense behind disassociating baptism from regeneration. Christianity is not magic. A person is not saved by reciting a specific incantation (sinner's prayer) or going through a certain ritual (the sacrament of baptism), yet the understanding of baptism as being essential to salvation is still an undercurrent in much of the church, logical or not.

This brings the discussion back to the issue at hand, namely, whether or not baptism is essential and intrinsically necessary to salvation. Biblically, it would appear that baptism is absolutely necessary. The command of Christ in Matthew 28, commonly known as the Great Commission, is to baptize people. Throughout Acts there is story after story of people being baptized. Interestingly, in Acts, there are three baptismal stories that happen in quick succession: the baptism of the Samaritans in chapter 8, the baptism of Saul in chapter 9, and the baptism of Cornelius and his household in chapter 10. If being born of water and Spirit is a mark of salvation, then these three stories give an important lesson. The Samaritans are baptized and then receive the Holy Spirit later when Peter and John visit. Saul receives the Holy Spirit at his baptism, which is seen in the parallel construction of "regain your sight" and "be filled with the Spirit/be baptized" in 10:17-18. Cornelius and his household receive the Holy Spirit and are then baptized afterward. Three different situations, all of them including baptism, and none of them happening in the same sequence. Especially enlightening for this issue of baptism being necessary, Cornelius was baptized after it was obvious he was accepted by God.

For all of the evidence within the Bible, however, there is still the logical objection that people can be saved without being baptized. One biblical story typically used to defend this idea is the story of the thief on the cross in Luke 23:39-43. There Jesus promised the thief that he would be in Paradise, but there was no baptism, so this is seen as biblical proof that baptism is not necessary. Because of the validity of that argument, the sacrament tends to be emptied of its theological importance even in congregations that celebrate it frequently. John Wesley had an articulate response for the issue of the necessity of baptism. He wrote in his Treatise on Baptism in 1756:

> It is true the Second Adam hath found a remedy for the disease which came upon all by the offence of the first. But the benefit of this is to be received through the means which he hath appointed; through baptism in particular, which is the ordinary means he hath appointed for that purpose; and to which God hath tied us, though he may not have tied himself. Indeed,

> where it cannot be had, the case is different, but extraordinary cases do not make void a standing rule.[4]

In other words, it may be that people can be saved by God without baptism, but people were commanded to baptize. So, while God may work without it, the church cannot work without it. And just because some can be saved without baptism does not mean that the church has the freedom or authority to forsake it as unnecessary. In reference to the thief on the cross, there are two issues with this passage as proof that baptism is not needed. First, it was impossible for this thief, or anyone else in the Gospels, to be baptized into Christ because Christ had not yet died. Christian baptism is an incorporation into the life, death, and resurrection of Jesus Christ. Because Jesus had not yet died or been raised on the third day, it would have been impossible for the thief to experience Christian baptism even if baptism were possible for him. Second, most Christians would have considered this unique case in the Gospel as one justifying the "baptism in blood" of a catechumen. It was actually still seen as proof for baptism!

As the sacrament is celebrated today, many congregations would do well to have an articulated understanding of what baptism is and whether or not it is necessary. It is not enough to have an official doctrinal statement; congregants must know what they believe and why. This is because many people, especially in the West, have access to writings and studies that are written by people who may or may not have the same theological understanding concerning baptism as that particular congregation's official belief. There are denominations, such as the Free Methodist Church, in which longtime members do not know that their official theological understanding of baptism allows for infant baptism, nor do they agree with it. There are other denominations and groups that have a convoluted understanding so that,

---

4   John Wesley, "Treatise on Baptism" (1756), in *The Works of John Wesley*, ed. Thomas Jackson (London, 1831; repr., Grand Rapids: Baker Books, 2002), 10.193.

while the denomination may officially believe in baptismal regeneration, the sacrament is celebrated like a public declaration of faith or an infant dedication with water. This can happen in denominations such as The United Methodist Church, where the official understanding is that baptism of both adults and infants regenerates the person baptized and they now have a new life in Christ by virtue of that baptism.

The key to understanding the issue of baptismal regeneration with respect to Wesleyan theology is that Wesleyans also understand that subsequent to baptism people can leave the faith. Once someone is baptized, that does not mean that he or she is automatically saved. Baptism itself is not a magic ritual that conveys something. Neither do people unconditionally persevere in the faith after baptism. Wesleyan theology recognizes the unfortunate reality that there are times when people can and do walk away from God even after a conversion experience in their lives. The life of faith after the baptism is what is most important. Baptism, however, is an essential part of that life of faith.

THE SACRAMENT OF HOLY COMMUNION

The sacrament of the Lord's Supper has created quite a bit of controversy in the life of the church, just as baptism has done. For this sacrament, there are four main practical issues over which well-meaning Christians disagree:

- What should be used for the Communion elements?
- How often should we celebrate the sacrament?
- Who is allowed to receive it?
- In what manner should we receive it?

These four debates, just like the three over baptism, have led to separations between Christians and divisions within the church.

Before moving into the debates concerning the Lord's Supper, we ought to take note of the scriptural references for the sacrament, just as we did with baptism.

INSTITUTION OF THE LORD'S SUPPER
Matthew 26:26-29
Mark 14:22-25
Luke 22: 14-23
1 Corinthians 11:23-26

CELEBRATION OF THE LORD'S SUPPER
Luke 24:28-32
Acts 2:42; 20:7; 27:36
1 Corinthians 10:16-21; 11:17-34

THEOLOGICAL MEANING
John 6:22-59

As you can see, there are far fewer references to the Lord's Supper in the Bible than there are to baptism. This is actually one of the major reasons there are so many disagreements over the sacrament within the church. This sacrament is supposed to be a time when the church can gather together and show its unity to itself, God, and the world. Yet with such a small pool of biblical texts from which to draw, when controversies occurred, it was difficult to appeal to the Bible as an external authority for a correct interpretation of meaning or practice. Therefore, we have the situation today in which there are significant differences in theology and practice with regard to the Lord's Supper.

What Should Be Used as Communion Elements?

The debate concerning what should be used in the Lord's Supper is twofold. One surrounds the bread and one surrounds the cup. Some churches use leavened bread (yeast bread) for Holy Communion and some use unleavened bread (wafers). Some use wine and some use grape juice. These differences do not seem to amount to much of anything, but they have been enough to keep faithful Christians from celebrating the sacrament together in the context of worship.

The issue of the type of bread is theologically complex, so we will look at that issue later in the chapter, in the "Theological Debates" section. The wine/juice issue is less complex but is still a real debate. For more than eighteen hundred years, there was never a discussion over the type of liquid used in the sacrament. It was wine.[1] Then, in the late 1860s, a Methodist layman named Thomas Welch perfected a way to pasteurize grape juice so that it would not ferment or spoil. He did this because he believed in the message of the temperance movement in America at the time, namely, that the abuse of alcohol was a plague on society and needed to be stopped. By creating a way

---

1 There is an interesting story of Francis Asbury, the famous Methodist preacher and bishop, who refused to celebrate the Lord's Supper at a church he visited on April 11, 1796, because someone brought brandy instead of wine for the sacrament. *Journal and Letters of Francis Asbury*, ed. Elmer T. Clark (London: Epworth Press, 1958), 2.82.

to mass-produce grape juice, Welch and his son had a way to enable churches across America to support temperance even in the context of worship with the Lord's Supper by marketing the juice as "unfermented sacramental wine."

From this point forward, denominations in America that held to the message of the temperance movement have used grape juice instead of wine for the sacrament. Besides the historical reason, they will also cite the ability for recovering alcoholics and children to participate in the sacrament without ill effects. Most congregations and denominations make their decision on the type of drink in the sacrament based on their own history, their primary recipients of the sacrament, and their own personal preference. Theologically there is no reason to prefer juice over wine or vice versa. There is a spurious claim that Jesus had grape juice at the Last Supper to try to support the practice of using juice in the sacrament, yet that is simply not true, as that meal was the Jewish Passover meal, in which a specific type of wine was used. There is no historical precedent for using juice before the 1870s, and thus, the practice of not using wine is a recent practice in the life of the church.

How Often Should We Celebrate the Lord's Supper?

Another aspect of the Lord's Supper that can divide well-meaning Christians is how often we should celebrate it and receive it. There are some churches and traditions that celebrate the sacrament weekly (or even daily). There are others who may celebrate it four times a year or less. We will examine some of the reasons for the difference in frequency of celebrating the sacrament in the "Theological Debates" section, but there are two main issues to discuss here: feelings of worthiness and sacredness.

One of the main objections to not receiving Holy Communion on a regular basis is that, based on 1 Corinthians 11:27-28, we are not supposed to receive it unworthily. This means that extra care and preparation are necessary before receiving the sacrament, and that kind of examination and preparation are only realistically done infrequently. There is a serious flaw in this kind of thinking, though. Paul wrote that we are not to take the sacrament "in an unworthy manner"; he did not use the word *unworthily*. No one is worthy before God to do anything. That is the point of the gospel, that Jesus did what we could not do so that we could stand before God. The issue at stake in this passage is whether those who receive it do so with an appropriate attitude toward the sacrament.

In Corinth, there were divisions among the Christians, and there was a divisive spirit that pitted one group within the church against another. As well, people were getting drunk during the meal that preceded the reception of the sacrament. The attitude of the gathering was anything but worshipful. In truth, the gathering looked more like a pagan feast than it did Christian worship. It is in this context that Paul wrote that the Corinthians ought not receive the Lord's Supper in an unworthy manner. If the sacrament is celebrated in a worshipful manner, this issue becomes moot.

The second reason many people feel as if the celebration and reception of the Lord's Supper ought to be infrequent is the issue of sacredness. In essence, the idea is that if the sacrament were celebrated frequently, it would lose its sacred quality and, as a result, come to be seen as a common thing. It would lose its special meaning in people's lives, and they would give it no more thought than they would eating lunch after church.

At first glance, this seems to be a logical argument. "Familiarity breeds contempt," as the saying goes, and having Holy Communion every week would make it into a boring ritual that would lose its holiness. Yet this is anything but logical. If this statement were true, why would we eat lunch every day after church? Why would we want to spend time with people to whom we have an emotional attachment (parents, children, spouses, etc.)? Why would we bathe on a regular basis? In each of these instances, we could make the same argument used against receiving Holy Communion: you would not appreciate food if you ate it frequently; you would cease to feel strongly for people you see on a regular basis; you would lose an appreciation for being clean if you cleansed yourself regularly. No, this objection is really not about sacredness at all, for who would not want to be in the presence of something sacred more frequently? Rather, this objection is about novelty. If the sacrament is celebrated frequently, the novelty of it wears off. This idea is based on a theological issue that will be examined in the "Theological Debates" section.

The biblical model for frequency of the Lord's Supper is not unanimous, but it is unanimous in advocating more frequency than many, if not most, Protestant churches in American today. Luke recorded the daily routine of the new church in Acts:

> They devoted themselves to the apostles' teaching and fellowship, to the breaking of bread and to the prayers. . . . Day by day, as they spent much time together in the temple, they broke bread at home and ate their food with glad and generous hearts. (2:42, 46)

The implication is that the believers were celebrating the Lord's Supper, even as part of a meal, every day. Later in Acts Luke wrote, "On the first day of the week, when we met to break bread . . ." (Acts 20:7). Here the implication is that the church celebrated the Lord's Supper weekly, on Sundays. Along with this reference is Paul's reprimand of the Corinthian church in 1 Corinthians 11. Here Paul wrote that when the Corinthians gathered together "as a church" (v. 18), which was weekly on Sundays, "it is not really to eat the Lord's Supper" (v. 20). This means that they were attempting to celebrate the sacrament weekly, but as Paul's chastisement continues, we find out that they were not celebrating it in a worthy manner, as just discussed. So, the biblical picture of frequency for the Lord's Supper is either daily or weekly.

Before we leave the frequency issue, though, there is one more objection to celebrating the Lord's Supper on a regular basis—it lengthens the worship service. There is anecdotal evidence from many different congregations across America that attendance on Communion Sundays is lower than the attendance as compared to other weeks. The main reason is that the service on those Sundays is lengthened to accommodate the reception of the sacrament. While this can be a real concern, the issue is not so much the sacrament as it is poor planning on the part of the pastor or worship team/committee for the time requirements for celebrating the sacrament and not allocating time accordingly for all the elements of the worship service.

Who Is Allowed to Receive the Lord's Supper?

The question concerning who is allowed to receive the Lord's Supper divides into two categories: non-Christians and Christian families. For many congregations that practice believers-only baptisms this becomes a singular issue, as they do not allow unbaptized people to receive the Lord's Supper at all. Thus, we will look at the issue of non-Christians and the Lord's Supper first.

The question about whether or not non-Christians can receive the Lord's Supper is not very complicated. Why would a non-Christian want to receive the sacrament? If there is no faith behind the motivation and desire, then the answer ought to be a forthright no. However, if there is a desire to be united with Christ and become a Christian, then the decision is a little more involved. There are some who would claim that someone would have to be a baptized and professed believer in Jesus Christ before he or she can properly receive Holy Communion, and there is a good case made for this position.

It is a case, with biblical support, for those who are not yet fully Christian to receive the Lord's Supper, however. The apostles were not filled with the Holy Spirit, a mark of being born again, until Pentecost. Yet they received the sacrament from the hands of Jesus himself on the night he was betrayed. These are people who made a commitment to Christ in faith, but could not yet be considered Christians in the truest sense of the word, because they had not yet experienced the benefits of Christ's death for them since Christ had not yet died. In the same way, the two disciples on the road to Emmaus (Luke 24:13-35) were not yet filled with the Holy Spirit but had enough of a commitment to Christ that they were saddened by his death. Yet Jesus himself offered them the sacrament when they got to the house. If people respond in faith, God will usually take care of the details.

The other debate concerning who can receive the Lord's Supper centers on children. How old is old enough for children to receive the sacrament? This is a particularly interesting question for churches that baptize infants and even for ones that dedicate infants. When can the children of believers receive Holy Communion? Some traditions and churches have decided the issue decisively and have no exceptions. The Roman Catholic Church allows children in second grade to receive the sacrament for the first time (First Communion), assuming this coincides with an age of reason to understand what the sacrament is and means in the life of a believer. The Eastern Orthodox Church administers the sacrament to infants immediately after being baptized; assuming that if one is a baptized member of the church, the Lord's Supper ought not to be kept from him or her.

The question then becomes one for Protestant churches and when they should allow their children to receive the sacrament. Should children receive Holy Communion as soon as they are physically able to receive it, or should they wait until they can understand what the meaning of the sacrament is, have made a profession of faith, and are spiritually ready? Much of this debate actually has much in common with the debate over whether or not infants ought to be baptized. Because much of the reasoning behind this question with regard to the Lord's Supper is theological in nature, the full treatment of this issue will be addressed in that section. Ironically, it is usually the Protestant churches with the least sacramental view of the sacrament, that of memorialism (discussed in the "Theological Debates" section), that have the most restrictive practices with respect to who receives it.

In What Manner Should We Receive the Lord's Supper?

There are two main ways people could receive the Lord's Supper, and they both are different ways of utilizing the cup in the sacrament. First, there is the method of having individual cups for each person receiving Holy Communion. This is a very popular way to celebrate the sacrament because people see it as more sanitary than using a common cup. It also has the added benefit for some congregations to look as radically different from the Roman Catholic celebration as possible, so that no one could accuse that particular congregation of anything deemed theologically improper. This is actually a symptom of a condition, colloquially called *Romaphobia*—the fear of anything that looks Roman Catholic.

With the practice of using individual cups for Holy Communion, people can make a further distinction in reception by either passing the cups out to people on trays in their seats, almost like a reverse offering collection, or the people can be invited to come forward to the front of the church to receive their Communion elements, usually kneeling at a railing. There are symbolic benefits to either of these two methods of receiving the sacrament. For the former, the case can be made that Christ comes to us and meets us where we are in life. For the latter, we have to move out of where we were in order to receive Christ as he is offered to us. Either way, the individual cups lead to a highly individualized and individualistic understanding and experience of the sacrament.

The second main way people receive the Lord's Supper is with a common cup, traditionally called a *chalice*. In fact, until the 1890s there was no celebration of the Lord's Supper any other way than with a common cup. The common cup was received by each person drinking from it. One after another, Christians would come up to someone holding the cup and take a small drink. While today this seems like a recipe for spreading sickness, it is important to remember that the liquid in the cup was wine, with an alcohol content that would kill many germs. As well, if the common cup were a breeding ground for illness, then clergy in churches that still receive Communion in this manner would be the sickliest people on the planet, since tradition dictates that they have to finish whatever is left in the cup, yet they are not so.

To help alleviate some of the health concerns over drinking from a common cup, some churches instituted receiving the Lord's Supper by a method known as *intinction*. This is when the bread is dipped into the cup and both elements of Communion are received together. Ironically, this method of receiving Communion is very close to the ancient (and current) practice of the Eastern Orthodox Church. In that church, the bread is placed into the chalice and the people are given a little piece from a spoon held by the priest or deacon.

Theological Debates

The questions surrounding who can or cannot receive the Lord's Supper or how it should be received or what should be used for the elements are all secondary, though, and flow out of the main theological issue regarding the sacrament: What actually happens during Communion? This is a question that has been debated, more or less, for the last eleven hundred years. Until five hundred years ago, the debate was less; with the Reformation, it became more. At issue is how Christ is or is not present in the sacrament. Broadly speaking, there are only two opinions concerning this issue. Either Christ is really present within the sacramental act or Christ is really absent within the sacramental act. All of the various theological opinions about the Eucharist are variations on these two positions. Because the principle of *lex orandi, lex credendi* holds true, which position a particular congregation or denomination holds on this issue will determine, to a great degree, how those Christians will include the sacrament within its worship.

Contrary to the established pattern in this book of looking at the earliest days of the church through today, what is called "real absence" will be discussed first. This is because this theological position is a minority position within the church. Even though it seems to be dominant in much of Western Christianity, it is the one theological understanding that has the least acceptance within the church. Many of the materials that are published explicitly for Protestants adhere to this understanding because some of the most popular companies in America that distribute Christian literature hold this position. Yet the abundance of books and resources in recent years does not mean that it is widespread.

The first person to put forth the idea that Christ was in no way, shape, or form present within the Eucharist was Ulrich Zwingli (1484–1531), a reformer in modern-day Switzerland and a contemporary of Martin Luther. As Zwingli progressed in his ideas and reform movement in Zurich, his understanding of the Lord's Supper was that Christ could not be present within the sacrament because his body was enthroned in heaven. If he was in heaven, there was no way Christ could also be within the elements for Communion. The sacrament itself was a metaphor for the Spirit of Christ being with the believers, and he took the words of Christ, "This is my body," to mean "This *represents or signifies* my body." The theological position that holds to this understanding is called *memorialism*, as the rite is a memorial of what Christ did for the community of believers. This was a radical departure from the major theologies that were contemporary to Zwingli, as well as the theological positions that came after it. In fact, memorialism is rejected by the official theologies of the Roman Catholic Church, the Eastern Orthodox Church, Oriental Orthodox churches, all Lutheran denominations, the worldwide Anglican Communion, most Methodist churches and Presbyterian churches, as well as any of the other ancient churches, such as the Assyrian Church and the Church of the East.

The reason so many churches reject memorialism as a proper theological interpretation of the Lord's Supper is because of the earliest teachings of the church concerning the sacrament. From the first generation of Christians that wrote concerning the sacrament, there was an understanding that Christ was truly present within its elements.

Ignatius of Antioch, in his *Letter to the Smyrnaeans*, wrote, "They [Docetists] abstain from the Eucharist and from prayer, because they do not admit that the Eucharist is the flesh of our Savior Jesus Christ, the flesh which suffered for our sins and which the Father, in His graciousness, raised from the dead."[2] This was written around AD 112. Ignatius was the bishop in Antioch, the same city in which the followers of Jesus were first called "Christians" (Acts 11:26). It was also this city that knew the ministries of both Paul, as this was the congregation that sent him on his journeys and to which he always returned, and Peter, who, according to Galatians, spent some time there as well (2:11). For Ignatius to be the leader of that congregation within the next generation of believers means that he was approved by those who learned the faith from those first apostles and others like them. This one statement is the strongest theological argument for Christ to be present within the sacrament both for its conciseness and for its proximity to the original apostles.

Besides Ignatius, there are dozens more references to Christ in the sacrament moving forward in the history of the church. Justin Martyr, Irenaeus of Lyon, Clement of Alexandria, Cyprian of Carthage, Athanasius of Alexandria, Cyril of Jerusalem, Hilary of Poitiers, Basil the Great, Gregory of Nyssa, Gregory of Nazianzus, John Chrysostom, Ambrose of Milan, and Augustine of Hippo all believed that the Eucharist was the actual body and blood of Christ. This is a veritable Who's Who of the ancient church, with some of its greatest minds represented on this list. What is most interesting about them, and the list could be much larger still, is that they all took essentially the same approach to the sacrament. They considered it a mystery. This is only logical, since the Greek word that was translated into Latin as *sacramentum* was literally *mysterion*. How Christ was present was not known; that he was present was completely affirmed.

---

2   Ignatius, *The Epistle of Ignatius to the Smyrnaeans*, in *ANF*, 1.89.7.

This idea of mystery is still the official understanding of the Eucharist in the Eastern Orthodox and Oriental Orthodox churches to this day. In the West, under the guidance of Rome, a more technical explanation arose within the church: *transubstantiation*. Perhaps it is because of the cultural conditioning of the Latin mind-set, but the Roman Catholic branch of the church was not satisfied with merely appealing to mystery for the explanation of Christ's presence within the sacrament. Rather, theologians in the West wanted to answer the question of exactly how Christ was there. As the theological inquiries, writings, and debates occurred over the centuries, the position at which the Roman Catholic church arrived was officially understood to be transubstantiation.

As a term, *transubstantiation* had its earliest potential reference from Justin Martyr in his *First Apology* written around 155. In it he wrote:

> Not as common bread and common drink do we receive these; but in like manner as Jesus Christ our Savior, having been made flesh by the Word of God, had both flesh and blood for our salvation, so likewise have we been taught that the food which is blessed by the prayer of His word, and from which our blood and flesh by *transmutation* are nourished, is the flesh and blood of that Jesus who was made flesh.[3]

Here the term *transmutation* is as close as the church was to using transubstantiation until the eleventh century, when the term first appeared. The Fourth Lateran Council in 1215 used the term to officially describe what happened in the sacrament, and finally Thomas Aquinas gave precise theological meaning to the term as official Roman Catholic dogma. The doctrine of transubstantiation is that the entirety of the bread and wine used in the Eucharist is changed into the body and blood of Jesus Christ. While this transformation is full and complete, the elements themselves still look and taste like bread and wine.

---

3   Justin Martyr, *First Apology*, in *ANF*, 1.185.66.

This is a form of grace given by God to the church so that people do not perceive flesh and blood in the sacrament. This became the official position of the Roman Catholic Church in 1215, and it is still the official position of the Roman Catholic Church today.

One aspect of this theology, and it is one with which the Reformers had the most difficulty, was that if Christ was physically present in the sacrament, then the Mass itself became a sacrifice. While some took this to mean that Christ was re-sacrificed at every celebration of the Mass, the official Roman Catholic theology was and is quite different. In its theology, the Roman Catholic Church taught, and still teaches today, that the Mass is a re-presentation of the sacrifice of Christ. In other words, the Mass commemorates what Christ did, but in such a way that those present at the Mass mystically become those in the upper room at the Last Supper and those at the foot of the cross the following day. This is the same concept as the Jewish practice and understanding of celebrating the Passover. No matter where or when in the world a Jewish family celebrates Passover, as the ritual is done and the meal is eaten, that family becomes one of the families delivered out of slavery in Egypt on the night of the last plague. So it is with the Mass and the celebration of the Eucharist. Of course, official dogma and personal piety and understanding are often two very different things. While this may have been the official teaching, and it is an understanding that could be welcome in most Protestant churches today, the practical understanding by most people was that the priest re-sacrificed Christ every day the Eucharist was celebrated. That idea was quickly rejected in the Reformation.

As the Protestant Reformation was beginning, two different understandings of the Eucharist arose. One, discussed earlier, was Zwingli's memorialism. The second was Martin Luther's view, which today is known as *consubstantiation*. In this view, Christ is physically present in the sacrament, but so is the bread and wine. Just as Jesus Christ had both divine and human natures, the elements in the Eucharist have two natures: of Christ and of regular food. Luther did not so much as change the idea of transubstantiation but ameliorate it. In Luther's understanding, it was plainly obvious that the bread and wine remained bread and wine, yet he fully believed that Christ was physically present in the sacrament, based not only on his own experiences, but also on the wealth of ancient Christian writings and tradition concerning the presence of Christ in the Eucharist. Thus, Luther concluded, both bread and Christ must be present. Luther answered the objection of Zwingli's point that Christ was enthroned in heaven with the concept of *ubiquity*, the idea that because Christ is God and God, by definition is everywhere, Christ's body could be in every Eucharistic celebration.

John Calvin tried to create a moderating position between both Luther and Zwingli. In Calvin's understanding, Christ was present in a spiritual sense when the church gathered together to celebrate the Lord's Supper. Those who gathered in faith experienced the virtue of Christ's presence among them. Because of this concept, his understanding was known as *virtualism*. On the one hand, virtualism recognized the very real problem with Christ's body being enthroned in heaven as Zwingli taught. On the other hand, virtualism also took very seriously the experience of Christ's presence among the people and the long history of theological writing on the subject of the Eucharist. Ironically, however, Calvin was so emphatic that Christ's presence was spiritual alone that the case could be made that the church could receive the presence of Christ without actually receiving *Communion*. The fact that Christians gathered together in faith expecting to receive Christ was enough for them to experience receiving Christ. It was irrelevant whether or not they actually consumed the bread or wine.

The Anglican Church, trying to stay in the via media between Protestantism and Catholicism, had a different understanding yet beyond these. The Church of England had a theological understanding that took the best parts of Calvin's virtualism and wedded it to the best parts of the historic understanding of the church. In the classic Anglican understanding, Christ is spiritually present in the sacrament (virtualism), yet it is through the elements of bread and wine that the spiritual presence of Christ is communicated to the people gathered. Something actually happens to the elements that transforms them from mere bread and wine into the vehicles by which Christ shares his presence with his church. The bread and wine are changed and Christ is truly present within them, but it is after a spiritual manner rather than a physical manner. Because John Wesley was a faithful Anglican priest, this is the theological understanding of the Lord's Supper that he bequeathed to the early Methodists, and it is still the theological view of the majority of Methodism to this day.

Depending upon a particular congregation or denomination's understanding will greatly impact how they celebrate the sacrament. For those who follow Zwingli and his understanding, it is highly probable that the Lord's Supper will be celebrated infrequently. The only reason to celebrate it would be to remember what Christ did for the church in the past. There would be a sense of gratitude and possibly commitment to Christian living, but ultimately the act itself becomes something that the church does simply because Christ commanded the church to do it. For those who follow one of the traditions that understand Christ is truly present in the sacrament, celebration of it will most likely occur more frequently, usually once per month or even weekly. The sacrament itself becomes one way the church can experience the presence of Christ anew and individual Christians can be strengthened in their relationship with God.

And this comes back, then, to the issue of who should be able to receive the sacrament. Many Protestant congregations and denominations who hold to a Zwinglian understanding of the Lord's Supper will restrict reception of it to only those who have been baptized. Because this view tends to coincide with having a believers-only understanding of baptism, this restricts the reception of the sacrament to only those who have made a conscious choice to follow Christ. Nonbelievers, seekers, and unbaptized children of baptized believers are not allowed to receive the sacrament because the sacrament is a historical remembrance of Christ's sacrifice and a present sign of membership in the community Christ founded. Just as baptism would not be appropriate for those who did not self-proclaim belief, so too the Eucharist would not be appropriate for those who were not already a part of the fellowship.

Ironically, many who hold a theological position that teaches that Christ is present in the sacrament in some way do not place so many restrictions on the reception of it. To be sure, some Protestants who have a strongly held belief in Christ's presence in the Eucharist will not allow nonmembers to receive it, such as more conservative branches of the Lutheran Church; others hold to a more open table position. The open table, or open Communion, is the practice of allowing anyone who would wish to come forward and receive the Eucharist. There are two main variations on this practice. One version allows any baptized person to receive the Lord's Supper, regardless of denominational or nondenominational membership. The other version allows any person, baptized or not, to receive the Lord's Supper.

Many Wesleyan/Methodist ecclesial bodies have some form of an open table. This is because Wesley himself believed that the Lord's Supper could be what he called a "converting ordinance." Wesley came to this conclusion in the late 1730s and early 1740s as he was debating the role of the sacraments in the life of a seeker or believer. It was, as he defended his position, that all persons should avail themselves of all of the means of grace (sacraments included) no matter where they were in their own journey with God, and he included a story about a woman who testified that she experienced saving grace and faith during her reception of Holy Communion. Wesley said, "What is to be inferred from this undeniable matter of fact—one that had not faith received it in the Lord's Supper?"[4] For Wesley, salvation was a dynamic and living relationship with God. That meant that any and all persons ought to put themselves in the spheres of God's working,

---

4   Wesley, *Works*, November 10, 1739, 19.121.

even if it meant receiving the Lord's Supper before they had faith. Because of this theological legacy and understanding about salvation, many Methodist denominations today allow anyone who seeks more of God to receive the sacrament.

There is one interesting theological and practical issue that arises out of this practice, though. In Wesley's day, almost 100 percent of the people who were Methodists were already baptized. They had been baptized in the Church of England as infants. Whether or not they had a saving faith, like the woman Wesley referenced, they were already nominal members of the church. This becomes interesting because many people today who do not have a saving faith are not baptized and are not members of any church. Using Wesley's experience as precedent and theological justification, many Wesleyan/Methodist denominations have found themselves administering the sacraments in reverse of the historical order of baptism and then Eucharist. Because of the open table, all are invited. Those who experience God's grace in the Lord's Supper then are encouraged to be baptized. Perhaps this is a modern missionary adaptation of praxis, but more theological investigation is needed in this area. There is still further work to be done on this issue.

9

MUSIC IN WORSHIP

Worship has always contained music. The Psalms collected in the Bible were composed to be sung in worship at the temple or in synagogue settings. The written account of the Last Supper notes that Jesus and the disciples sang a hymn as they went out from the upper room after the meal. Paul even wrote to the Ephesians and Colossians that the Christians were to "sing psalms, and hymns and spiritual songs" (Ephesians 5:19; Colossians 3:16). This portion of worship has transformed over the centuries, yet with a few exceptions, it has always been an important part. Recently, especially within what is commonly called contemporary worship, the music portion of the service is exclusively referred to as *worship*, and the song leader or band leader is called the worship leader. This leaves the prayers, scripture, sermon, and sacramental acts outside of the definition of *worship*. Obviously, no serious Christian would deny those other elements were an integral part of worship, yet this language has persisted. It would be categorically wrong to refer to only music as worship, and care ought to be taken to correct this misconception whenever it is encountered.

Despite not being the sum total of worship, music is important. With the Wesleyan revival of the eighteenth and nineteenth centuries, many have rightly pointed out that more people were sung into the kingdom than were preached into it. There is little wonder as to why this is true. Charles Wesley wrote more than nine thousand hymns, most of which were deeply theological in nature and able to be sung to tunes that did not take a professionally trained choir to sing. It was due to the efforts of people like Charles Wesley, Isaac Watts, Fanny Crosby, and others that entire generations of Christians learned their theology through song. Because of these developments it is difficult to imagine Christian worship without music in some form within it. Unfortunately, something that has been so ubiquitous in worship for the church has also become extremely divisive within congregations in recent history.

Music in the Early Church

There is not much historical record of music within the context of worship in the biblical period or shortly thereafter. Part of the reason for this absence is the same reason there is not much written concerning the sacraments in worship: no one had to write about something that was happening everywhere. As noted in the beginning of this chapter, there are scant references to music within worshiping communities in the New Testament. The only reference to singing during the earthly ministry of Jesus is the hymn after the institution of the Lord's Supper in Matthew 26:30 and Mark 14:26. Because psalmody was intrinsic to Jewish worship, it is reasonable to assume that these faithful Jewish men and women who were with Jesus would have sung psalms when they worshiped in the temple and in the synagogue. Yet it is frustrating for students of worship and students of history not to have an explicit reference to this occurring.

The next mention of singing, which most likely confirms the assumption that the early Jesus movement did sing in worship, was from Paul in his letters to the Corinthians (1 Corinthians 14:26), Ephesians (5:19-20), and Colossians (3:16). While they are not sung per se in the text, there are also the New Testament canticles. A canticle is simply a song in the biblical text that is not contained in the Book of Psalms. In the Old Testament there is the song of Hannah in 1 Samuel 2:1-10 as well as the apocryphal Prayer of Azariah, which recorded the song sung by the three young men when thrown into the fiery furnace in

Daniel 3. The Gospel of Luke contains the three New Testament canticles. First, there is the Song of Mary, or the *Magnificat*, which is the first word of it in Latin, in Luke 1:46-55. Second, there is the Song of Zechariah, which is known by its first word in Latin, *Benedictus*, in Luke 1:68-79. Finally, there is the Song of Simeon, which is known by its Latin name, *Nunc Dimittis*, its first words, in Luke 2:29-32. These three canticles are composed just as songs would have been in that culture and day. As a result, while there is no record of them being sung in any of the biblical communities, there is ample record of these canticles being sung in worship services from early dates after the first century.

Beyond these references to singing in Paul and these three canticles in Luke, there are other recorded instances of singing. One was when Paul and Silas were in prison in Philippi (Acts 16:25). In this passage, Paul and Silas were said to be "singing hymns to God" while they were chained and awaiting what would happen next. Another reference to singing is in James 5:13, where James recorded that if any of the Christians to whom he wrote were happy, "they should sing songs of praise." Finally, there are several songs recorded in Revelation that point to the importance of music and singing within worship in continuity with both the Old Testament and the new covenant community in the church.

Singing was an integral part of Christian worship, yet there is little beyond these recorded instances that explicitly states that the church sang when it gathered. Again, no one needed to write down what everyone else already knew. The earliest proof of this fact comes from Pliny's letter to Trajan, written around AD 112. As Pliny was torturing Christians to discover exactly what seditious acts they were committing, he found "that on an appointed day they had been accustomed to meet before daybreak, and to sing a hymn antiphonally to Christ as to a god."[5] There are scant references to singing after this incident,

---

5   *A New Eusebius*, 19.

although it is not long after Pliny's persecution that some of the most ancient hymns still in use were first found in Christian writings. One of these hymns is the *Phos Hilarion*, most likely composed in the 200s. This was the hymn sung in the evening when the lamps were lit in the sanctuary during a vespers service. The fact that new hymns and songs were composed for use in worship shows that music and singing were important components of worship. Near this time is when the *Gloria Patri*, also known as the Lesser Doxology, was composed. As well, *Gloria in excelsis Deo*, the Greater Doxology, was composed near this time or even earlier.

Music in the Medieval Church

After these early developments of music within the church, more and more songs were written. In the East, there arose a system of eight tones to which a hymn could be set. This is still the form of hymnody in Orthodoxy today. There are a few different types of hymns that are composed in Orthodoxy, and each type has its own unique variation on the eight tones, but these are the only musical settings appropriate for music in worship within those congregations.

There is some debate as to the origin of Western chant, known as Gregorian chant. Tradition holds that it was Gregory the Great, pope at the turn of the fifth century, who created this form of music for worship. The tradition is that while Gregory was the papal ambassador in Constantinople, he was exposed to the Eastern form of chant. When he was recalled to Rome and made pope, he fused this Eastern form with Western modes of music and created a new form of chant. Whatever the source of Gregorian chant, what is certain is that it was the dominant form of music in worship for centuries. It supplanted other forms of chant that were already being used in other places around Europe. Despite the hegemony Gregorian chant held within worship in the West, other forms of music developed and eventually flourished. Many of these forms were the precursors to the modern music widely known in the West today. These included the use of instruments, which was significantly different from chant since it was sung a cappella. As well, there was the introduction of music that harmonized different voices, called *polyphony*. Chant is *monophonic*, which means it has only one melody. Polyphonic music, on the other hand, allows different voices to sing different notes at the same time. This would ultimately become the music known today, with different parts singing and harmonizing simultaneously. Also, during this era the organ was first introduced to congregations as a way of accompanying the singing during worship.

The history of music for this period of time is quite convoluted. There were several different currents all running at the same time, and only sometimes in the same direction. Gregorian chant took on a more harmonic way of singing, thereby creating two different versions of it. One was monophonic and one was polyphonic. There were congregations that had instrumentation in the service, and there were congregations that continued with the more ancient and traditional practice of singing a cappella. There were even hymns written in vernacular languages, mostly in Germany, that were used not only as a means of worship but also as a means of discipleship. This was because the hymns were used to teach new converts the truths of the Christian faith, as opposed to the songs of worship to their former gods.

Music in the Reformation Church and Beyond

All of this background moves the discussion to more familiar ground concerning music in worship for most Protestants. When the Reformation occurred, two different opinions were birthed. One was typified by Martin Luther and the other by Ulrich Zwingli. Luther believed that whatever was not explicitly denied in the Bible was permissible for the church. Zwingli believed that whatever was not explicitly approved in the Bible was not permissible for the church. As a result of these differences, numerous issues were never resolved in Reformation bodies.

One of those issues was music in worship. Luther had no problem using hymnody to increase lay participation within a worship service. He used new compositions in the vernacular to teach doctrine, and he was a strong proponent of instrumental music in a service since it was what the people knew. Zwingli, however, saw no reference to instruments being used in the New Testament for worship. Therefore, based on his theological opinion above, since he could not prove instrumental music for Christian worship from the Bible, there was to be no instrumental music for Christian worship in his congregations. New music was composed, but it was all a cappella.

Two centuries after the start of the Reformation, the Wesleys began the Methodist movement, a movement that was centered as much on music as it was on sacraments and preaching. In this aspect they inherited the tradition of hymn writing from other reformers before them. There was such an emphasis on singing within Methodism that one of the terms by which members of this movement were known was "singing Methodists." The Wesleys wrote and published several hymnals during their lifetimes, and many of these underwent several editions. One collection they produced early in the life of the movement was *Hymns on the Lord's Supper*, a collection of 166 hymns composed by Charles in 1745. It underwent nine editions by 1786! The Methodist movement produced several hymnals in its early years, mostly because they understood the value of singing as a way of teaching doctrine to people through a medium that was more memorable than simple teaching. The first hymn in almost every hymnal published by Methodists to this day was and is "O for a Thousand Tongues to Sing."

The Wesleys and the Methodists were not alone in this understanding of music as a tool for discipleship within the context of worship. From the 1500s forward, there was an explosion of musical composition for use in worship. Luther wrote numerous hymns and published multiple hymnals. John Calvin, more in line with Zwingli's understanding of what was appropriate in church, published a metrical psalter that included all of the psalms along with canticles and musical settings for other texts of scripture, such as the Ten Commandments. The Puritans had a psalter and hymns. The Quakers wrote hymns. The Baptists composed thousands of hymns. All of this was even before 1800. Once the Second Great Awakening began in the United States around the beginning of the nineteenth century, there would be yet another explosion of songwriting for use in worship, with thousands upon thousands of spirituals, songs, and hymns.

In recent history there has been yet another explosion of composition of music for worship in churches. Unlike previous generations, though, this movement today is not confined to any one particular theological tradition. With most of the newer hymns and songs being not only published but recorded and broadcast, people from all of the various traditions within the church are exposed to the same music. In addition, with Christian music now an industry of its own, where writing and performing is a career, there are fewer theological checks and balances before music is released to the public. As a result, just as in all eras before now, there are hymns and songs that are well composed and teach theological truths as well as songs that are neither well written nor practical for teaching.

The Hymnal

Because of so much musical composition occurring down through the centuries, the best and easiest way to get the music in the hands of the people was by publishing it in hymnals. From the earliest days of the Reformation, hymnals served as a way for these new churches to increase their adherents' knowledge of God and reinforce their piety. By giving the people access to worship music, the church reiterated the concept of the priesthood of all believers, as anyone could participate in worship at any time. The hymnal became an invaluable resource in the growth of the new church and its members.

The irony of all of this hymn writing is that, relatively speaking, very few of these hymns are known today. Most of the pre-Reformation music is totally foreign to the average congregation, and well over 90 percent of the music composed from the 1500s through the 1800s is lost to the church. This is primarily due to space limitations. While hymnals were wonderful tools to put theology set to music in people's hands, there were only so many hymns that could be included in any given book. Each particular individual or denomination had to make a judgment as to which hymns would be included in the current hymnal. This meant two things. First, each song within that particular hymnal would be vetted for the message and theological content within it. A Methodist hymnal would not usually include a song that taught a theology of predestination. A Reformed congregation would not use a hymnal that sang of a general call for all of humanity to respond to God. Lutherans would not sing Eucharistic hymns that were Zwinglian in nature. The hymnal was a filter so that the theology sung by a congregation would be congruent with that congregation's stated beliefs.

Second, only the best songs would be included in the hymnal. As the old saying goes, the cream rises to the top. Most hymnals had a few hundred songs in them. That is a small percentage of the total number of songs written for worship throughout church history. The majority of songs and hymns that were written have simply passed into history, with only the absolute best songs still being printed in hymnals today. This was a good development. Many of the songs and hymns that are no longer published or known today needed to be forgotten. Many of them simply did not convey theological truth, or did so in such an awkward way when put to music that they were extremely difficult to sing. With this pattern of only keeping the best songs, for all of the songs that have been written since 1980, perhaps five will still be sung two hundred years from now.

While the usage of physical hymnals has been on a decline in the Western context, the principle of the hymnal and its benefits can be restored. The current situation in many (if not most) congregations in the West is that physical books are no longer used, as lyrics are projected on some type of screen or video monitor for the congregation to see. This development has caused many denominations to cease publishing hymnals or the redefinition of what constitutes a "hymnal" in a digital era of internet and cloud-based technology. Yet even if a particular congregation utilizes an exclusively digital format for their musical repertoire, there is still the problem of placing the sung theology in the hands of the people. In instances like these, it might behoove those congregations to publish a list of hymns and songs that are theologically congruent with the congregational or denominational theology. It could be either in physical form or also digital. This would help members discern what Christian music would be most appropriate for their background.

Advice for Choosing Music for Worship

What this means for a current setting in worship today is clear. The older songs that are still known today have stood the test of time. They are the ones that the church has recognized as being of value to teach, edify, and comfort its people. These songs ought to still be used within the context of worship precisely because of this fact. The newer songs are still being vetted for their efficacy within the life of the church. While some of the music may be emotionally effective, an equal emphasis must be placed on the theology the song teaches (or does not teach, as the case may be). This is because of the principle of *lex orandi, lex credendi*. The theology that is sung will be learned and accepted more readily than the theology that is heard. Because the current field of compositions is presently in the process of being vetted, officially by leaders and unofficially by everyone, it is important to remember that just because the song is popular now does not mean it will stand the test of time. For people who have the responsibility for choosing music for worship services, use the same rule of thumb in choosing music as for using a metaphor in trying to explain the Trinity: try to be as least heretical as possible. As this happens, the newer songs and hymns that will stand the test of time will continue while the others will fall quietly to the wayside.

When choosing music for a worship service, it is of the utmost importance to remember two main things: the theological tradition of the congregation and the focus of worship. As individuals or groups try to piece together hymns or songs for a worship service, the theology taught by the song must be considered. It is not enough that the song or hymn contains a phrase that is similar to a point in the message or theme for that particular service. The other lyrics may teach a theology that is radically different from what the congregation believes or needs to hear. Coupled with that idea is that the focus of worship is on God, with the people of God singing praises to the One who is worthy. Much of the newer music actually has people, not God, as the focus of the song. While the tunes may be memorable and the message may even be biblical, those songs would be more appropriate for personal devotion and general edification, not worship.

Choosing particular hymns and songs for worship is an important responsibility and must be done with prayer and discernment. The principle that people will learn their theology as they sing it is absolutely true. This means that the selection of worship music is just as important, or more so, than the sermon in any given service. With that kind of a responsibility, it is vital that the music not simply be chosen because it is currently popular. Likewise, it is critical that music for worship is not chosen because it is thought that "this will bring people in to church." That would be an evangelistic motivation for a song. Evangelism is people-focused. Worship is God-focused. If a service is created and planned for the purpose of bringing in new people, it is an evangelistic service, not a worship service.

One of the major practical outcomes of considering worship music in this fashion is how the role of worship leader/pastor is construed. Just as there is a difference between worship and evangelism, so too there is a difference between a worship leader and a band leader. Musical talent should never be the sole criterion for the role of worship leader. Musical talent and a relationship with God also should not be the only two criteria. If a person is going to effectively teach theology set to tunes, that person must have a strong knowledge of the theological tradition of that particular congregation and be able to effectively communicate that theological tradition in words and song. The worship leader position within a congregation is intimately tied to the discipleship process of that congregation.

If a congregation published a list of Christian music that is appropriate for its theological background, a local "hymnal" as described at the end of the previous section, further distinction could be made within it for discipleship purposes. Holding true to the principle that worship ought to be focused on God, there could be a further distinction in the "hymnal," whether physical or digital, as to which songs are most appropriate for worship and which songs are most appropriate for other settings. By taking the time to teach congregants the principle of *lex orandi, lex credendi*, a congregation or denomination could reinforce a deeper theological understanding of worship and help create a new generation of Christians who understand the intimate link between stated beliefs and how those are embodied within a congregational setting.

10

OTHER SERVICES

The majority of this book has focused on what happens in a typical worship service, by whatever name it is called: Sunday service, main service, worship. There are many, many more services in which congregations participate over the course of a year, and there are many more opportunities for individual Christians to use a "service" for their own private devotional experiences. This is nothing new. Even in Acts 2, as the newly enlarged church set about in worship, the believers met together every day in homes as well as meeting at the temple. As the movement spread across the Roman Empire and beyond, multiple services were instituted and passed along to new communities, new congregations, and new generations of Christians. Many of these services continue to follow the basic pattern of drawing close to God so that God can draw close to people, and thus are worship services. Yet these are also services that were never seen as the main service, most for obvious reasons. Following are a few of those services that are still practiced in some form or another today.

Prayer Services

According to Acts 2:42, one of the four key elements the early church taught its new converts was *the prayers*. These prayers are never explicitly stated, but it is obvious that the Lord's Prayer, the Our Father, was included in that set of prayers. Extremely early in the life of the church, across multiple different locations and in various cultures and languages, prayer services began as a part of the life of the worshiping communities. The Book of Acts itself has several references to people who were followers of Jesus praying at specific times throughout the day. Each of those times was an established time of prayer from the Jewish tradition these believers either knew or inherited as disciples of Jesus. The miracle of Pentecost happened at 9:00 a.m. in Acts 2. Peter and John went to the temple in Acts 3 at "the hour of prayer," which was 3:00 p.m. In Acts 10 Cornelius was praying at 3:00 p.m. when an angel came to him. Peter was praying at noon when he received his vision from God. Cornelius's household received the Holy Spirit at 3:00 p.m. Paul and his companions met Lydia outside of Philippi at the hour of prayer in Acts 16. When Paul retold his conversion story in Acts 22, he recounted that Jesus appeared to him at noon. Each of these instances involved a Jewish time of prayer, and even Jesus's crucifixion corresponded to them, as he was crucified at 9:00 a.m., darkness came over the land at noon and lasted until 3:00 p.m., and Jesus died at 3:00 p.m. It was only natural for Christians to carry these hours of prayer over into their own lives.

Along with these hours of prayer, there were also the morning and evening sacrifices and prayers at the temple that the Christian movement inherited. Every day there would be a service and a sacrifice for the community near dawn and dusk. It was natural that these services also were included in Christian life as time progressed, and especially after the legalization of Christianity, when worship was intentionally modeled after temple worship. What arose from this period was a schedule of a morning and evening service that was usually communal in nature. The early service was called *matins* (or *orthros*) and the late service was called *vespers*. These two services became fixtures in the life of the church, and remain so to this day in many traditions. They were designed to be celebrated in community, in the main worship space of a congregation. Vespers is from such an early period that one of the oldest hymns still known, written sometime in the early 300s (or possibly even earlier), is *Phos Hilaron*, known in English as "Hail,

Gladdening Light." It was composed as a lamp-lighting hymn for the vespers service.

The other hours of prayer were incorporated into private devotional times of prayer throughout the day. Eventually, by the 500s, Benedict of Nursia systematized a pattern for individual prayer that spanned nine different points throughout each day:

Matins—Lauds (3:00 a.m.)
Prime—First hour (6:00 a.m.)
Terce—Third hour (9:00 a.m.)
Sext—Sixth hour (noon)
None—Ninth hour (3:00 p.m.)
Vespers—Evening Prayer (usually 6:00 p.m.)
Compline—Night Prayer (9:00 p.m.)
Nocturns—Vigil (midnight)

This scheme was created for monastic usage, for monks and nuns who lived in a monastery or convent and devoted themselves to prayer for the better portion of their lives. In modern usage, and in most congregational usage outside of monasteries or convents, matins and lauds (and sometimes even terce) are combined into one morning service.

John Wesley, being an ordained priest in the Church of England, practiced morning and evening prayers on his own as a private devotional practice. In 1738 he published a prayer book that gave a form, devotional material, and self-examination questions for morning and evening prayers for every day of the week. Over the last two hundred years of Methodism's history, there have been various emphases on morning and evening prayer in the different branches of the tradition. Today, the *Book of Common Prayer* still retains the morning prayer, noonday prayer, evening prayer, and Compline. Methodism, following its ecclesiastical parent, the Church of England, has forms for morning praise and prayer, midday praise and prayer, evening praise and prayer, and night praise and prayer in The United Methodist Church's *Book of*

Worship.[1] All of the services are designed to be used either privately in a devotional sense or corporately as a worshiping community, although the preferred usage is in community with one another. The midday and nighttime prayers are simpler and shorter than the morning and evening services, and thus can used more easily in a private way as well. There are countless other resources on prayer, both corporate and private, from many different denominations, in print today.

These prayer services, whether done corporately, as a family time of prayer, or individually as private devotional times, still conform to the essential pattern of worship. There is a time when the person or group draws near to God through prayers of preparation, reciting a creed, reading scripture passages, or even a short reading from someone in church history. Then there is also a time for intercessory prayer and waiting upon God. Both movements are present in these prayer times, and there are even ample opportunities for music and extemporaneous prayers built into many of the orders for the services. The only time these services can be misused so that they do not conform to the basic pattern of worship would be when they are presented either rapidly or without time to pause to hear from God. If an individual or group is using the prayer service simply to "get it done," the point is missed and it may do more harm than good in the lives of those who experience it.

Even though these services can follow the basic grammar of worship, they should not be used as a replacement for corporate worship, where the emphasis is upon the entire community meeting to praise God, be edified through the reading of scripture and its exposition, encouraged through a call to deeper commitment and discipleship, and have an opportunity to receive from God more of the grace needed to live the life of faith in the world today. A prayer service has a time for people to draw near and experience God drawing near to

---

[1] See Appendix B.

them, but it does not have the full range of what is included in an actual worship service.

Weddings

Wedding services are most often wonderful times of celebration. They are a sign of a new beginning of love and relationship. They are filled with hope and faith that the future will be blessed. The services themselves also take the form of worship, either specifically for the couple being married or for the entire group that has gathered to celebrate the marriage. Obviously, those being married are not completely focused on what happens during the service, so care ought to be taken before the wedding ceremony to explain to the couple exactly how this is a form of worship.

Someone once said that marriage is like martyrdom. To have a healthy Christian marriage, each person has to die to himself or herself for the sake of the other. Because Christians know that the only way to truly live a life of self-sacrificial love is by the grace of God, this becomes an important aspect of the wedding ceremony. Depending on local tradition for specifics, there are several aspects of a Christian marriage ceremony that are overarching. The two being joined in marriage declare for themselves that they desire to be married to one another. Sometimes there are symbols that are used to signify the marriage. The most traditional symbol is a ring to be worn by one or both of those who are now joined together. Often, a candle is lit by both individuals to show unity, or two different colors of sand are poured together into a large glass jar to represent the comingling of them in this new family. After those symbols, the officiating minister asks for God's blessing and grace to be given to this new couple as they endeavor to live a Christian life together. The couple draws near to each other and to God, and God is invited to draw near to them. Worship.

It is also somewhat common to celebrate the Lord's Supper at a wedding. This gives not only the couple an opportunity to experience

God drawing close to them, but for all those who are present to have that same experience. Because many people who attend a wedding may be adherents of another faith tradition or have absolutely no faith at all, care must be used to explain the meaning of the Eucharist if it is to be celebrated. Despite that concern, Holy Communion is a most appropriate way to celebrate a wedding. Not only does the sacrament look back to Christ's crucifixion, but it also looks forward to the Marriage Supper of the Lamb at the end of all things, when God and humanity will dwell together forever as creation is restored. In this way, every Christian marriage can become an icon or a foreshadowing of the hope inherent in the Christian faith. As well, since the Lord's Supper was the traditional way that Christians experienced the presence of God drawing close to them, it is a most fitting addition to a Christian service that reminds the church of the union between Christ and them.

Funerals

A service of death and resurrection is an essential service within the Christian faith. The church proclaims to follow one who defeated death, and therefore, death no longer has any power over its members, nor do they have any fear of death. And yet death is an ever-present reality in every congregation and in every family. To make sense of the physicality of death in a theological way and to bring comfort to the brokenhearted loved ones who are left behind after a death, funeral or memorial services are necessary.

It can be more difficult to see a funeral as a worship service, but it is an occasion for those who gather for the service to draw near to God. This is true whether the one who passed was a living saint and the service is truly a celebration, or if the one who passed was not so saintly and there is much grieving. The reality is that while Christian theology professes that death is not the end of life, for as long as these loved ones live the deceased will be absent from their lives, and that is worthy of grief and sorrow. So, those in attendance draw near to God for comfort and sometimes to try to understand why the death occurred. This portion of the basic grammar is easy to understand. The more difficult portion is how to provide space and time for God to draw near to the people.

One traditional way clergy have provided for God to draw near to people is to give an invitation to follow Christ at the funeral. This is a practice that was popular in the nineteenth and early twentieth centuries in the United States, especially among more of the Holiness tradition churches in the Wesleyan/Methodist family. It is still regularly seen in other traditions and in other places around the world. After seeking to provide comfort for the family and friends of the deceased by explaining the reality of Jesus Christ's victory over death and what that means for every follower of his, an opportunity is given for those who are not yet followers of Christ to seek God's grace and transformation in their own lives so that they can be assured of resurrection to eternal life themselves. This provides a space and time for God to draw near to those who would like to experience the presence of the Holy Spirit in their lives.

There are two drawbacks to this option, especially if it is used exclusively as the opportunity for God to draw near to the people. First, this type of altar call at a funeral has been manipulated in the past so much that it has become a caricature in many regions in the North American context. Second, even if it is done well, this only provides an opportunity for those who are not yet in a saving relationship with Jesus to experience God drawing close to them. There may be many people in attendance at a funeral who are lifelong, faithful Christians who need that space and time as well to experience God's comforting grace. By exclusively using a call to discipleship as the opportunity for God to draw close to people, many of those who need that assurance and comfort will not experience it. Another option for creating that space and time in a funeral service is to have a concerted time of prayer that is more intercessory for those who are mourning and to direct the prayer so that it is obvious that its intended focus is not so much on the deceased, but on those who are left behind. There could be an appropriate time of silence so that people have the opportunity to experience God's Spirit bearing witness with their spirits of God's presence and grace.

Love Feast

This service is very much a part of the Wesleyan/Methodist tradition. John Wesley experienced the love feast while he fellowshipped with the Moravians both during his stay in Georgia and after his return to England. It was a common part of their devotional life together, and Wesley incorporated it into the life of the Methodist movement even after he and the Moravians parted ways in 1740. In the earliest decades of Methodism, the love feast was one of the primary services in which people experienced the power and presence of the Holy Spirit. It was usually held quarterly (usually coinciding with a full moon so that those in attendance would have ample light to walk home after dark), and only Methodists in good standing could attend the service. In fact, doorkeepers were appointed to check whether or not each person arriving for the service had a class ticket, which was required for entry. The class ticket was only given to those members of a society who faithfully and regularly attended their class meeting and were active in seeking to live according to the General Rules of Methodism. If people did not have their class tickets, even if they were enrolled as a Methodist, they were not allowed to attend this service.

The love feast itself was nothing more than some songs, prayer, scripture verses or a passage, symbols of fellowship, and testimonies. The symbols of fellowship were bread and water. The reason water was used was so that no one could confuse the service with the Lord's Supper. In an era when the overwhelming majority of Methodist preachers were not ordained, and thus did not have any sacramental authority, the distinction between the love feast and the Lord's Supper was essential. No Methodist could be accused of trying to usurp a sacramental role, nor could the Methodists be accused of trying to form their own church separate from the Church of England, because this was not the Eucharist.

The reason for the closed nature of the service was that it was focused heavily on the transforming work of God in people's lives. The testimonial portion of the service was where people experienced the grace of God in almost unprecedented ways for that time in England. Stories were shared of how God had been at work in people's lives, giving them victory over sin and temptation, assurance of salvation, and even the experience of sanctification. As the testimonies were shared, they gave confirmation to the preaching of God's grace available for all, which was one of the hallmarks of the Methodist movement. The testimonies were seen as encouragement for those beginning the journey, exhortation to those on the journey, conviction for those who had backslidden on the journey, and ultimately examples of God's grace and presence for the journey. The testimonies were always accompanied by prayer and a time of deep intercession for those present and loved ones absent from the meetings to experience the same kind of transformation and victory.

Today there are several iterations of the love feast throughout the various worship manuals and resources of the different Wesleyan/Methodist denominations. Some of the orders for the service are very close to what the earliest Methodists experienced; some of them are more updated. This is a service that still has a place within worship today. It is best experienced if it is not done on a regular basis, but done frequently enough that those in attendance are familiar with the order of the service and what to expect. If introducing the service for the first time, it is best to walk the people through the entire service with words of instruction and commentary, even for the little things of the service. It would also be helpful if the entire text of the order of service, along with some words of direction, could be made available before the service to those who will attend. That way they can be familiar with some of what will happen and can focus on the experience of the service rather than the novelty of it. If part of the service selected includes the option of people speaking words of scripture as they pass the bread to the next person, it would be most helpful to have several appropriate scripture verses printed for people to choose from. That way no one would feel inadequate if he or she did not have scripture memorized or simply could not recall something because of the newness of the experience. It would also be best to have a way for all in attendance to clean their hands before the service, as everyone takes the loaf of bread and offers it to the person next to them. Finally, make sure there are tissues or cloths available for those who are moved to tears either by giving a testimony or hearing one, or during the prayer time afterwards.

Covenant Renewal Service/Watch Night Service

Another unique contribution to worship from Methodism is the Covenant Renewal Service, also known as the Watch Night Service. Because Methodism believed that those who were in a saving relationship with God could backslide and let go of that relationship, and because the purpose of Methodism when it arose was to spur people on to holiness of heart and life, Wesley incorporated a Covenant Renewal Service into the life of the Methodist movement. He probably borrowed the idea of an evening service from the Moravians, just as he borrowed the love feast, but the unique development he contributed was the focus on covenant and renewal. The Covenant Renewal Service was similar to the love feast in several ways, with singing, prayer, and testimonies. Yet it was distinct from the love feast in two important ways. First, there was no bread or water associated with this service. Second, the focus was on the covenant made between people and God. It was an opportunity for people to rededicate their lives to living as Christians in the world and seeking as full an experience of salvation as possible. As such, the Covenant Renewal Service was only held once per year, usually when John Wesley visited a particular society. In time, the service came to be celebrated almost exclusively on New Year's Eve, which is why it is also known as the Watch Night Service today.

When celebrating the Covenant Renewal Service, one of the best ways to create a more meaningful time of worship and covenant is to have individual copies of the service, or at least the covenant prayer, for each person present.[2] These copies should then also have a place for the people to sign their names. In this way the seriousness of the covenant may be made more real. Once people have affirmed the covenant, prayed the covenant prayer, and signed the covenant, there should be time to spend in prayer before God, seeking help and grace to live out what was just renewed. Whether the service is done on New Year's Eve or some other day important to the life of a particular congregation or community, it should be an annual event. It should be a time of introspection, taking the seriousness of the covenant prayer to heart, and it should be a time of celebration and joy, remembering that it is by God's grace that anyone is able to live in relationship with God, and that it will be by God's grace that the covenant that was just reaffirmed will be upheld.

Visitation of the Sick

Worship can happen in a church building, or it can happen in a hospital room. There are some places in the world that have a more sacred character and feel to them, but the triune God is in all places. One of the most meaningful moments of worship can be when people need to be assured of the presence of God around them, as is the case when they are sick. This time of intimate worship with a few people can be even more powerful and deep than in a regular worship service. Whether the minister follows a specific, written form for prayers with the sick or prays extemporaneously, remembering the two essential parts of the basic grammar of worship will help. Give people the

---

2   See Appendix C.

opportunity to draw near to God. This can be done through an initial prayer, by reading portions of scripture, and by inviting honest conversation about the person's spiritual state. Then, give people the opportunity to experience God drawing near to them. This can be done through more direct intercessory prayer, allowing the person to pray himself or herself (either silently or aloud), giving Holy Communion to those present, and/or anointing people with oil for healing.

Practically, if the Eucharist is to be given and anointing oil used, these elements will need to be brought to the one who is being visited. In addition, if there is a portion of a liturgy that will need to be used for any of the visit and it requires responses, copies will need to be provided for those who are present. Finally, if anointing oil is used, make sure there is a way for the one who did the anointing to clean the oil off of her or his hand after it is used. Because many people in the United States do not have much experience with oil used in the context of prayer or worship, some teaching may need to be done before the visit or some words of explanation may be needed at the visit before the anointing. Even if that teaching has taken place before the visit, if family members or friends are present, some words of explanation may be appropriate. It is always best to explain what is going to happen before it happens than to try to explain why an action was taken. It allows those who may not be familiar with a particular aspect of the Christian faith and practice to either observe or participate from a position of knowledge rather than confusion. As with any aspect of worship, it will mean more to people if it means more to people.

11

PRACTICALITIES

Throughout this book there have been numerous references to what is done in worship, when, and by whom, the nouns and verbs of the grammar of worship. However, the objects used for various purposes in worship were only briefly discussed, if at all, in previous chapters. This chapter is meant to balance that issue by giving a more thorough treatment of those objects, the things used in worship. Depending on the theological tradition of a particular congregation or denomination, some of these objects will be used and some will not be used. Some congregations place more theological importance on certain ones than on others. Some hold the objects themselves as more sacred than others. Nevertheless, all congregations have certain tools they use to help facilitate worship. Remember: different aspects of worship will mean more to people if they mean more to people. In other words, no matter which of these items are used, or what form they take, explain them and their meaning to the congregation periodically. Do not assume the congregation will learn simply by being present, and do not reduce the meaning to the point where it becomes simplistic and devoid of any real theological meaning. Worship will take on new meaning and new depth for worshipers if they understand the reason behind what is included in the church building for worship, what happens in worship, and why.

Altar/Communion Table

This, quite simply, is a table. It can be wood or stone or even a folding table. It may have words inscribed upon it or symbols carved in it, or it may be plain. Practically, its function is to be a flat surface upon which the elements for Holy Communion can be placed. Theologically, it becomes a symbol itself of God's love for humanity. In congregations where the sacrament is celebrated on a regular basis, it is usually very visible each time the people gather. Often it is in the center of the chancel area. Some congregations place a large Bible on it, usually open and resting on a stand so it is more vertical and the congregation can see the pages. Someone once said that a Communion table with an open Bible on it shows that neither is used very often. That Bible serves as a decoration, or even an icon, but is rarely used to read scripture in a service. Likewise, if the table has a Bible on it, there is little room for the elements for Holy Communion. This may be a healthy critique of such decorating.

Candles are frequently placed on the altar table as well. Often there are two candles, one on each side. Aesthetically, this is a visually pleasing arrangement because it provides symmetry to the table. Theologically, two candles have been used to symbolize the dual nature of Christ as all God and all human. The flames on the candles also symbolize Jesus Christ as the light of the world as well as the presence of the Holy Spirit, who appeared as a tongue of flame on Pentecost. Some congregations have more ornate candles, and some use three, symbolizing the Trinity, or four, symbolizing the four Gospels, or seven, in imitation of the seven-branched candle stand from Revelation (itself a carry-over from the menorah of Jewish worship). If the congregation uses candles in worship, it is preferable to have a candle lighter, usually used by an acolyte. This is a brass tube into which a skinny taper is placed. There is no specifically liturgical reason why this item is to be used other than the fact that it can be lit and then used to light multiple candles, rather than using either a lighter or match each time a candle needs to be lit.

Some congregations make it a practice to place the tithes and offerings on the table after they have been collected. While actually taking up a monetary collection is an ancient practice, both advocated by Paul in 2 Corinthians and attested to by Justin Martyr in Rome one hundred years later, the practice died out when Christianity became the official religion of the Roman Empire. After that point, the church was financially supported by the state. This was a common situation throughout even the Reformation, as Protestant churches also became local state churches. As such, collecting an offering is actually relatively new in the life of the church. And yet, even in those periods when the church was financially supported by the state, Christians still brought offerings to their respective congregations. Often these were in the form of food for the poor or the bread and wine for the Eucharist. Because these offerings come from the people and are for the furthering of the kingdom of God, either in worship or in ministry beyond the walls of the church building, it is theologically appropriate to place them on the altar table in an act of thanksgiving and consecration to those purposes.

Altar Railing

Chapter 3 discussed the railing around the main chancel area. There it was pointed out that it is variously called an altar railing, Communion railing, or prayer railing. In the Holiness tradition it is also called, somewhat erroneously, the altar. This piece of furniture can have a profound impact on the life of a congregation. It originally was created to separate the area for the clergy from the area for the laity within the worship space, yet it can be a holy location in and of itself. Leaving the issues of clericalism aside, this railing serves as a reminder of the design of the temple in Jerusalem. There, different precincts were separated from one another and moved to a progressively more holy location. This railing can now serve as a reminder to people that God is holy and distinct from the rest of the world. Yet it is also a reminder that Christians are called to be a holy people. As such, the railing becomes a place where the people who are called to be holy can meet the holy God. In the Celtic tradition, it is a thin space where God and humanity interact.

In some traditions there is a practice of an altar call, in which preachers invite people to come forward after a sermon and offer themselves to God in a moment of conversion. This is where the term *altar railing* originated. In a conscious effort to distance themselves from this practice, which was often seen to be emotionally driven and even manipulated in the past, many congregations who still have this piece of furniture in their worship spaces do not use it in the context of worship at all. A healthy theology of prayer and a significant time of teaching of the purpose of this railing can bring this powerful accoutrement of worship back into use in many places. After all, if the railing is designed to bring to remembrance the temple, that building was supposed to be "a house of prayer."

Baptismal Font/Baptistery

Baptism has always been a part of the Christian tradition. Consequently, there has always been a need for places to be baptized. In the earliest days of the church, baptisms happened outside, in rivers, lakes, and seas. As time progressed, congregations built areas specifically for baptisms inside buildings. The earliest church building in Dura-Europos had a room set aside for baptisms, with a baptistery that was large enough for an adult to enter and have water poured over his or her head. From there baptisteries were built either as a part of the main worship area in a particular building, or as a separate section to the building, or even in a separate building itself once church structures were legal and became larger and more ornate. As more and more infants were baptized, it also became common to have a baptismal font, a raised bowl that would hold enough water to pour over a baby's head.

The design of these baptisteries and fonts often had theological significance. Many of them incorporated the number eight into their design. If the baptistery was in a separate building, that building was often eight-sided. If it was in a separate portion of the main building, that section was often eight-sided. Sometimes even the pool was an eight-sided pool. Baptismal fonts are often eight-sided. The reason for the prominence of the number eight with respect to baptism is because of the theological meaning behind the sacrament. Christians are baptized into the death and resurrection of Jesus Christ, and Christ was resurrected on the first day of the week—the eighth day. Keeping the week time frame from Genesis in mind, that would put the resurrection on the first day of a new creation. Through baptism, the Christian is brought into that eighth day, the first day of the new creation.

Likewise, these baptisteries and fonts were very often at the back of the worship space, or in a separate place altogether. The reason for this was that it was only through baptism that one truly became a Christian. Faith and experience were not enough; one had to make the journey through the waters of deliverance to enter into the promised land of the church on the other side. Baptism served as the boundary between the fallen world and the new creation. It was the rite to experience and the border to cross in order to enter into fellowship with the people of God. For this reason, it was physically removed from the front of the worship space to symbolize the journey a person travels from death to life, sin to salvation, exile to return. Today many baptismal fonts are placed outside of the communion railing for a similar reason. Baptism is the means through which Christians approach God. For church buildings that install baptisteries today, theological concerns rather than ease of sight by the congregation ought to govern where it is placed.

Communion Vessels

Because there are various ways to celebrate the Eucharist, various kinds of vessels are used in the sacrament. Depending on the type of bread offered, a plate or a stack of trays will be needed. If a plate is used, either for Communion wafers or bread, it is most appropriately called a *paten*. This can be metal or earthenware, and it usually matches what is used for the cup in the Lord's Supper. The cup itself can also either be a stack of trays, if individual cups are used, or a single cup called a *chalice*. Whatever the utensils and whatever the form for the sacrament, great care ought to be taken to ensure the proper attitude toward the celebration of the sacrament. It is a holy moment in a worship service and should be treated as such. For congregations that use the wafers for bread, one other vessel may be used: a *ciborium*. It usually matches the chalice in design, and is essentially a bowl with a lid. It is used to hold the wafers before the service, and sometimes after the service is concluded if there are more left than were used.

Icons

Icons, statuary, paintings, and other images are often used in worship, although statues are usually not found in Wesleyan/Methodist congregations. Even in congregations that do not approve of the use of images in worship, crosses are still on walls, stained glass windows are installed, and often projector screens are used to help facilitate worship. Images are useful tools in worship precisely because the contemporary culture is a highly visual one. If care is taken to explain the right way to utilize imagery in worship, it can become a great benefit to the worshiping community.

Iconography, specifically of the Eastern Christian tradition, can be especially useful within the context of worship. Not only is there a well-described theology behind the icons themselves; the current culture of the West is one that is foundationless and unrooted. By using ancient paintings to help tell a biblical story or by highlighting an example of a model Christian from history and having a painting of that person, it can help reinforce the reality that the church is rooted. It is a way to help people who feel lost in a sea of options know that the ship of faith has withstood the test of time. Again, simply having old-looking pictures will not cause this reality to be known. It will take teaching on the subject to communicate the truth behind it.

Incense

While not used in many congregations in the Wesleyan/Methodist tradition, some congregations do use incense as another way to engage all the senses in worship. The United Methodist Church's *Book of Worship* included an option for the use of incense in the Order for Evening Praise and Prayer. The use of incense in Christian worship dates back to the legalization of Christianity by Constantine in the fourth century AD. Before this, most (if not all) Christian congregations did not use incense in worship, because it was associated with pagan offerings and Jewish worship. Once Christian worship became legal, the use of incense was introduced. This was not without biblical precedent. Incense was commanded to be used by God in worship at Mount Sinai. It was used in temple worship. It is promoted in Psalms. And it was seen in Revelation in heavenly worship. Given these instances, it was easy for the church to adapt its worship and include something that was biblical. This is especially true given the fact that Christian worship at this time intentionally modeled itself on Jewish temple worship in its architecture and other accoutrements.

Biblically, incense is equated to prayer; therefore, one of the main places of use is during prayer. This is why it was included where it was in the *Book of Worship*. If being used during prayer, it is enough to have a lit charcoal in a bowl that will not break due to heat. Special coals are made specifically for liturgical function. At the time of prayer, a piece of incense can be placed on the charcoal and the smoke and aroma will rise up, giving a visual and olfactory sense to prayer.

In more liturgical traditions, incense is also used to mark something as sacred or holy. In instances such as these, the bowl for incense also has a lid and is on a chain that can be swung toward the object that is to be marked. Again, the smoke and the scent give an added dimension to the concept of blessing. It is also important to note that objects such as the Eucharistic elements are often blessed, and so is the worshiping congregation. The people themselves are marked as holy as they gather to worship God.

Lenten Objects—Pyx and Tenebrae Candles

Ash Wednesday is a service that is celebrated more and more in Protestant churches today. Where once it was thought to be almost an exclusively Roman Catholic observance, many Christians across the liturgical and theological spectrum now see it as a wonderful way to begin Lent. It gives the appropriate seriousness to the church season and is a wonderful contrast to the glory and joy of Easter Sunday. For congregations that wish to observe Ash Wednesday with ashes, a *pyx* will be necessary. A pyx is nothing more than a dish to hold ashes. Traditionally the palms from the previous year's Palm Sunday service are saved and burned to make the ashes although, more and more, ashes are available to order from supply houses. To help the ashes stick to the people (in the places they are supposed to stick!), it is necessary to mix them with something. Do not use water! That will make an almost irredeemable mess. Mix a little olive oil in the ashes. Use just enough to make a very light sludge. Then, when the people come forward, a thumb lightly pressed into the ashes collects enough to make a decent cross on the forehead. The pyx itself could be something designed specifically for this purpose. There are actual dishes that are made for this, both of metal and earthenware. Or it could be a small dish that will not detract from the solemnity of the occasion. Make sure a towel is available for those who imposed the ashes immediately after that portion of the service has concluded so they can clean their hands.

Another item that may be used in worship during Lent is a candle stand for a Tenebrae service. *Tenebrae* means *darkness* and was designed to convey the fight between light and dark during the end of Jesus's earthly ministry. This service is most appropriately held either on Holy Thursday (Maundy Thursday) or Good Friday. The service should begin at night, or at least very close to sundown. The service itself is a series of readings, mostly from the Gospel of John, that tell the story of Jesus's trial and crucifixion from Gethsemane to his burial. The story is divided into sixteen different readings, and fifteen candles are needed for the symbolism of the service to have its fullest expression. Fourteen of the candles should be the same size and color. The color is optional, but purple, the liturgical color of Lent, or deep red are most appropriate. (Do not use black candles; that would make the service look evil.) The fifteenth candle should be a different size and color, preferably white. A candelabra or some other vessel will be needed to hold the candles. It is best if the fourteen candles are all in the same type of holder. If a congregation does not have enough candlestands, or multibranched candlestands, one can be made out of wood, with holes drilled into it to hold the candles. The fifteenth candle should be among the others, but separate from them.

As each of the readings is done, one of the fourteen candles is extinguished. In this sense, Tenebrae is a reversal of lighting the Advent wreath, where the light gradually increases as the congregation gets closer and closer to the Christmas celebration. Now, as the service progresses, the congregation experiences increased darkness. This is why it is most appropriate to celebrate this service when it is already night. Also, as many of the lights in the worship space should be turned off as possible, increasing the darkness and setting the tone of the service. Because the fifteenth candle represents Christ, it is not extinguished. It is hidden after the second-to-last reading, symbolizing Christ being buried and hidden in the tomb. This service is most visually meaningful and symbolic if it is paired with stripping the sanctuary, the practice of removing everything from the worship space that can be moved that has a symbol of Christ on it, and the service of light on Easter, where everything that was removed is brought back into place along with candles, bringing light back into the sanctuary.

Pulpit/Lectern

The *pulpit* is a piece of furniture where the preacher may rest the Bible and sermon notes. Usually it is a large stand, either made of wood, stone, or some other material. For much of church history, the preacher would deliver the message from the pulpit. In many congregations today, it is a free-standing piece of furniture, but centuries ago it was a fixed portion of the church building, often raised up above the rest of the room. In instances like this, the preacher was said to "go up into the pulpit" to preach. Traditionally, the pulpit is placed at the center of the chancel area in a Protestant congregation, which shows the centrality of preaching for that tradition. A *lectern* is a similar piece of furniture, but often not as large or ornate as a pulpit. It is the stand where much of the Bible readings are done; hence, the term from lectionary. This means that the lectern is associated with the written word while the pulpit is associated with the spoken word. In congregations where both a lectern and a pulpit are present, they will many times be on opposite sides of the chancel area, with the altar/table between them. This is called a split-chancel arrangement.

There has been a growing practice among congregations to eliminate the pulpit (and lectern) altogether, or replace them with a simple music stand. Much of the impetus of this movement was to make the worship space look less "churchy." For congregations that make this decision, it should not surprise them when their members see no distinction between what happens during worship and what happens everywhere else in the world. There is a reason we understand a sacred/secular divide. The world is still in process of being redeemed, and church is the vanguard of that redemption. As such, it has always been different from the rest of the world. As the church moves into the world, it spreads the kingdom of God and makes it more sacred. By trying to emulate the rest of the world, many congregations have brought the secular into the sacred space. It is not surprising, then, that congregations see no difference between the kingdom and the world.

If that is the theological position and tradition of a particular congregation for worship, great care should be taken to ensure that the congregation understands the difference between the kingdom of God and the rest of the world. The converse is also true, however. Just because something looks out of the ordinary does not necessarily mean congregants will understand the distinction. Remember: worship (and all aspects of it) means more to people when it means more to people.

Robes/Vestments

Specialized clothing for those having a specific role within worship began at some point in history, but like most developments in the history of Christian worship, it is not clear precisely when because people did not write about something that was widespread or known by almost everyone. Certainly, after the legalization of Christianity, clergy and servers wore distinct garb during services. More than likely the practice was done well before this point, although most definitely the robes were not nearly as ornate. The purpose of using robes, stoles, and other specialized articles of clothing within the context of a worship service has two main aspects. First, the clothing was to take the emphasis off of the individual and place it upon the person's function. This is also described as hiding the person within the calling of Christ. Second, and related to the first, is that the differences in specific aspects of the clothing designated what unique role a person had in the service. A bishop had different vestments than a priest. A priest had different vestments than a deacon. A deacon had different vestments than an acolyte. They all had similarities in their clothing, but there were certain idiosyncrasies for each role.

Today, there is still a distinction in vestments between the different roles, or orders, within the church. While the vestments of the ancient churches, Roman Catholic and Eastern Orthodox, can be quite complex, most Protestant churches (and certainly those within the Wesleyan/Methodist family that use vestments) use the stole to signify the difference between persons in worship. The stole is a mark of ordination. It is variously interpreted in history as the yoke of Christ being taken upon the person ordained, a towel or cloth that a slave would have to serve all people, or even Aaron's beard full of anointing oil for ministry. Bishops have symbols unique to their office upon their stoles, the shepherd's crook and the ship of faith. Within Methodism that is the only distinction between them and elders, as bishops are seen as a specialized ministry within the Order of Elders. Each elder has a stole that drapes around the neck and falls in front over both shoulders. Deacons may use a stole that drapes across the side from the left shoulder to the right hip, much like a sash. Those who are not ordained but serve in various roles within the worship service, such as acolytes or unordained preachers, do not have stoles. The common exception to this distinction is choir robes, which have a stole of sorts, but it is designed in such a way that it cannot be confused with those designating ordination.

As far as the robes and stoles are concerned, there are various colors. Most of the stoles are created with some variation of the liturgical color of the season. In that way the clergyperson may coordinate with the church calendar with respect to dress. This is an ancient practice that dates back to the earliest records of vestments. The robe itself usually is one of two colors: white or black. Other colors usually have something to do with a local preference, academic degree, specific denomination, or some other factor. However, the vast majority of clerical robes are either white or black. White is reminiscent of the early practice of giving new Christians a white robe at their baptism. As such, it is the common robe for all baptized Christians. Within Protestantism especially, there is a tradition of using black robes for clergy. This dates back to the beginning of the Reformation and its removal of anything Catholic from the service. Since Roman Catholic priests used ornate vestments over a white robe, that mode of dress was eliminated. In its place the clergy would wear their academic robes, which, as is the case today for most schools, were black.

Many congregations today do not use vestments at all. There are a variety of reasons for desiring to use them and for not using them. As with all aspects of worship, it is important to first decide what the purpose of worship is, and then to seek guidance for how to best accomplish that task. Let the theology of the congregation and the congregation's tradition help form the reasons for using or not using vestments. The important point to remember in making such decisions, though, is that worship is not evangelism, and not wanting to look churchy is not a valid reason for making a decision.

Along with the issue of special vestments or robes within the context of the worship service is the question of special clerical dress outside of worship. There are three main ways clergy dress. The majority of Protestant clergy do not dress any differently than anyone else, specifically in the Western world and most specifically in the United States. Other clergy wear a clerical cassock, similar to a robe used in worship, but with a different design and function. This was the traditional clerical garb of the Roman Catholic and Anglican churches for centuries. It is still the traditional garb of Eastern Orthodox clergy in most places around the world today. The most recognizable form of clerical dress is the collar. This is a shirt, often black but also other colors, with a white collar that is either a tab in the front of the shirt or a white band that wraps completely around the neck. It was a Protestant invention as an alternative to the Roman cassock but was quickly adopted by Roman Catholic clergy. It is a typical vestment for Protestant clergy outside of the United States, and is becoming more popular in the United States for more and more clergy.

Again, the reasons for clergy to either dress differently or similarly to others outside of a worship service will vary. Some clergy dress in a distinctive way to remind people that the church is alive and well. Some clergy dress in a distinctive way to remind themselves for whom they are ambassadors in the world. Some clergy dress in a like manner to everyone else to show that holiness is not confined to a specialized group within the church. Others dress in a like manner to everyone else so they are incognito. There are other reasons as well, but whatever the decision on how clergy dress, it should be formed by one's theology, calling, and conviction by God.

Sanctuary Lamp

The sanctuary lamp, or eternal flame, is a candle, oil lamp, or even electric light bulb usually housed in a red glass. It is lit or turned on to symbolize the presence of God in the midst of the worshiping community. Biblically, its origin is traced back to Exodus 27 with the admonition God gave to Moses to never let a lamp go out before the Lord. This injunction is still practiced in Jewish synagogues today. In Christian theological traditions that reserve a portion of Holy Communion that was consecrated during a service, the lamp is usually placed near where those elements are stored. In other traditions the location of the lamp is typically toward the front of the worship space so it is easily seen by the worshiping community. While not essential to worship, many congregations use this as a way to visually remind themselves of the reality of the light of Christ in the world, much like the use of candles on the altar table.

CONCLUSION

The earliest Christians understood worship to be central to the Christian life. Generations of Christians after them have agreed. Worship is a key component of the life of faith, and it is an invaluable tool for discipleship. This has been seen century after century in the principle of *lex orandi, lex credendi*, the rule of prayer is the rule of belief. How Christians worship impacts their understanding of God, and their understanding of God informs how they worship. What is taught in studies and classes is reinforced to a much greater degree through the context of worship, and it is worship that provides the context for what Christians believe.

Worship is essential for the Christian life. Worship forms us as Christians, and it informs us of who God is and who we are in relationship to God. For worship to be able to fulfill this role, it needs to have certain elements. Just as a sentence must contain certain elements of grammar in order to make sense, so too worship must have certain elements. There are nouns, the people, places, and things of worship. These include people's roles within a service, the spaces set aside for worship, and the items used within the context of worship. There are verbs, the actions within a worship service and the order in which they occur. And just as sentences can be simple or complex, short or long, so too worship can be more complex and ornate or more direct. Nevertheless, what is necessary does not change.

For worship to be as full as it can be, there must be a time for Christians to draw near to God and a time for God to draw near to the people. These two movements are absolutely necessary for worship to occur. Throughout the majority of the church's history, people have drawn near to God through prayers, scripture, and sermon. The time set apart for God to draw near to the people has been the sacrament of the Lord's Supper. In the modern era, people still draw near to God through the original elements, but music now also plays a significant part in the service. The time for God to draw near to the people needs to be more clearly defined in many congregations. It can be the sacrament or it could be a focused time of prayer. However it is formed for various communities and congregations, worship should be an intentional time for people to experience the presence of God in a real and tangible way.

While trying to appropriately plan and implement a worship service, it is also essential to remember that worship, by definition, is not evangelism. Worship is God-focused. Evangelism is people-focused. Churches that confuse the two do neither well. The most balanced expression of the Christian faith will have a serious commitment to evangelism, reaching new people with the truth of the gospel message and the freedom it brings, along with a serious commitment to worship, the time when the people of God can gather together in a group to offer praise and thanksgiving as a response to God for that freedom and deliverance.

When the Wesleyan/Methodist movement began, there was a concerted effort to keep worship and evangelism in their proper places, and to have a strong emphasis on each. The Wesleyan revival of the eighteenth century was just as sacramental as it was evangelical in nature. For those congregations and traditions that are descended from that original revival, recapturing the centrality of worship and sacrament will be key in recapturing the momentum from those early days. In Wesley's day the Church of England had worship but did not have the transforming power of God. Wesley saw this as having a form of godliness without the power (see 2 Timothy 3:5). Today, in many congregations there is neither the form nor the power. Services are not even remotely connected with the essential elements of Christian worship, and there is no real transformation within the congregational life. God willing, this introduction will help congregations recapture the form. As those congregations grow, drawing near to God and intentionally seeking God's presence drawing near to them, they will also experience a renewal of the power. If that occurs, then we will be able to look at this quotation from John Wesley, not with lament over its prophetic truth, but with a godly admiration that we continue and persist.

> I am not afraid that the people called Methodists should ever cease to exist either in Europe or America. But I am afraid, lest they should only exist as a dead sect, having the form of religion without the power. And this undoubtedly will be the case, unless they hold fast both the doctrine, spirit, and discipline with which they first set out.[1]

---

1 Wesley, "Thoughts upon Methodism" (1786), in *Works* 9.527.

APPENDIX A
WORSHIP SERVICE WORKSHEET

Date _____

Scripture Reading(s)

_____

Potential Elements of Worship (not an exhaustive list):

Call to Worship	Hymn/Song	Responsive Reading	Creed
Unison Prayer	Pastoral Prayer	Lord's Prayer	Sermon
Offering	Peace	Baptism	Holy Communion
Announcements	Skit	Invitation	Confession

Draw Near to God

_____
_____
_____
_____
_____
_____
_____
_____
_____
_____

APPENDIX A

God Draws Near

_____
_____
_____
_____
_____
_____
_____
_____
_____

When choosing elements for a worship service, remember to answer the question, "What is the purpose of worship?" Also, remember to have elements in both parts of the service. They may not be equally split, but there must be a dedicated time not only for the worshiper to draw near to God, but also for worshipers to experience a dedicated time for God to draw near to them.

Examples of Worship Services:

Draw Near to God
Call to worship
Hymns/Songs
Unison prayer
Scripture/Sermon
Creed
Offering

Draw Near to God
Welcome/Announcements
Hymns/Songs/Video package
Offering
Scripture/Sermon

God Draws Near
Pastoral Prayer/Personal Prayer at railing
Lord's Supper w/time at railing
Invitation
Hymn/Song
Benediction

God Draws Near
Pastoral Prayer/Personal Prayer at railing/Anointing for Healing
Hymn/Song

Dismissal

Whether the dedicated time to seek God's drawing near to the people is liturgical, sacramental, or prayerful, it is a necessary component of worship. The sermon is not God drawing near. While it may contain a *fresh word* for people in the congregation, it is life application commentary on the Scriptures already given by God for humanity to study as they draw near to God. As such, it is most appropriate to be placed in the first portion of the service.

APPENDIX B
PRAYER SERVICES

The following Prayer Services are taken from The United Methodist Church's *Book of Worship*. They have been modified slightly from their original form. Other sources for prayer services include the *Book of Common Prayer* of the Episcopal Church, and *A Field Guide for Daily Prayer* by Seedbed. The following forms of prayer services may be adapted to be used in a family setting or for private devotional use. If used alone, simply read all of the call and response texts together. It is not necessary to change the pronouns from plural to singular, though, as these prayers are being offered by Christians around the world at all times in various forms. Even when Christians are alone, they never pray alone.

An Order for Morning Praise and Prayer

Call to Praise and Prayer
>**Leader:** O Lord, open our lips.
>**People:** And we shall declare your praise.

Morning Song or Hymn
>Any song or hymn that is appropriate to the morning would be suitable here.

Prayer of Thanksgiving
>The following, or something similarly thankful for a new day, is prayed, either by the leader or in unison.

New every morning is your love, great God of light,
and all day long you are working for good in the world.
Stir up in us desire to serve you,
to live peacefully with our neighbors,
and to devote each day to your Son,
our Savior, Jesus Christ the Lord. Amen.

Scripture

Scripture passages that pertain either to the morning or to a specific season of the year may be read. Lectionary readings for the coming Sunday may also be used, or a daily lectionary that has readings for weekdays may be read.

Silence

Silent prayer and meditation on the scripture read.

Leader: Let our prayers be acceptable to you, O God, our rock and our salvation. Amen.

Song of Praise

The traditional morning song of praise is the Song of Zechariah, the *Benedictus*. Any song, canticle, psalm, or hymn of praise is appropriate.

Prayers of the People

This time of prayer may be extemporaneous or it may be directed by a litany. If a litany is used, prompts are read aloud. Time is given for the people to either pray silently or offer names that fit that category. Then the leader closes that petition and the people respond with the following:

Leader: Lord, in your mercy,   or   Let us pray to the Lord
People: Hear our prayer.   or   Lord, have mercy.
Leader: Together let us pray
　For the people of this congregation . . .
　For those who suffer and those in trouble . . .

For the concerns of this local community . . .
For the world, its peoples, and its leaders . . .
For the church universal—its leaders,
    its members, and its mission . . .
In communion with the saints . . .

The Lord's Prayer

The Blessing
The grace of the Lord Jesus Christ,
and the love of God,
and the communion of the Holy Spirit
be with you all. Amen.

The Peace

An Order for Midday Praise and Prayer

Call to Praise and Prayer
Even youths will faint and be weary,
    and the young will fall exhausted;
but those who wait for the Lord shall renew their strength,
    they shall mount up with wings like eagles,
they shall run and not be weary,
    they shall walk and not faint.

Song or Hymn

Prayer of Thanksgiving
God of mercy, this midday moment of rest is your welcome gift.
Bless the work we have begun, make good its defects,
    and let us finish it in a way that pleases you.
Grant this through Christ our Lord. Amen.

Song of Praise

APPENDIX B

Prayers of the People

> **Leader:** Lord, in your mercy, or Let us pray to the Lord
> **People:** Hear our prayer. or Lord, have mercy.
> **Leader:** Together let us pray
>> For the people of this congregation . . .
>> For those who suffer and those in trouble . . .
>> For the concerns of this local community . . .
>> For the world, its peoples, and its leaders . . .
>> For the church universal—its leaders,
>>> its members, and its mission . . .
>>
>> In communion with the saints . . .

The Lord's Prayer

The Blessing

> **Leader:** The God of peace be with us.
> **People:** Amen.
>
> **Leader:** Let us bless the Lord.
> **People:** Thanks be to God.

The Peace

An Order for Evening Praise and Prayer

Proclamation of the Light

> **Leader:** Light and peace in Jesus Christ.
> **People:** Thanks be to God

Service of Incense

Incense has been used in Christian worship since at least the 300s, specifically linked to Psalm 141. If it is used, it is appropriate at this time to place a piece of incense upon a charcoal already lit before the service began. There are numerous liturgical supply stores that sell charcoals and incense specifically for Christian worship, as well as incense holders. Once the incense is lit, Psalm 141:1-2 is recited:

> I call upon you, O Lord; come quickly to me;
> > give ear to my voice when I call to you.
> Let my prayer be counted as incense before you,
> > and the lifting up of my hands as an evening sacrifice.

Evening Hymn

This is any song that will focus on the ending of the day. The traditional hymn for this service is "Hail, Gladdening Light," which is found in numerous versions ranging from Orthodox chant to a rendition by the David Crowder Band in 2009.

Prayer of Thanksgiving

> We praise and thank you, O God,
> > for you are without beginning and without end.
> Through Christ, you created the whole world;
> > through Christ, you preserve it.
> You made the day for the works of light
> > and the night for the refreshment of our minds and bodies.
> Keep us now in Christ; grant us a peaceful evening,
> > a night free from sin; and bring us at last to eternal life.
> Through Christ and in the Holy Spirit,
> > we offer you all glory, honor, and worship,
> > now and forever. Amen.

Scripture

Either scripture passages that pertain to the evening, or to a specific season of the year may be read. Lectionary readings for the coming Sunday may also be used, or a daily lectionary that has readings for weekdays may be read.

Silence

Silent prayer and meditation on the scripture read.

Song of Praise

The traditional evening song of praise is the Song of Mary, the Magnificat. Any song, canticle, psalm, or hymn of praise is appropriate.

Prayers of the People

This time of prayer may be extemporaneous or it may be directed by a litany. If a litany is used, prompts are read aloud. Time is given for the people to either pray silently or offer names that fit that category. Then the Leader closes that petition and the people respond with the following:

Leader: Lord, in your mercy,   or   Let us pray to the Lord
People: Hear our prayer.   or   Lord, have mercy.
Leader: Together let us pray
    For the people of this congregation . . .
    For those who suffer and those in trouble . . .
    For the concerns of this local community . . .
    For the world, its peoples, and its leaders . . .
    For the church universal—its leaders,
        its members, and its mission . . .
    In communion with the saints . . .

The Lord's Prayer

The Blessing

Leader: The grace of Jesus Christ enfold you. Go in peace.
People: Thanks be to God.

The Peace

An Order for Night Praise and Prayer

Call to Praise and Prayer

Leader: O God, come to our assistance.
People: O Lord, hasten to help us.

Leader: The Lord Almighty grant us a restful night and peace at the last.
People: Amen.

Night Hymn
Any song concerning the night is appropriate here.

Prayers of Confession
This may be corporate or individual, a litany or extemporaneous.

Silence

Song of Praise
This is usually a joyful psalm.

Silence

Prayer of Thanksgiving
As you have made this day, O God,
>   you also make the night.
Give light for our comfort.
Come upon us with quietness and still our souls
>   that we may listen for the whisper of your Spirit
>   and be attentive to your nearness in our dreams.
Empower us to rise again in new life to proclaim your praise,
>   and show Christ to the world. Amen.

The Lord's Prayer

Commendations
Leader: In peace we will lie down and sleep.
People: In the Lord alone we safely rest.

Leader: Guide us waking, O Lord, and guard us sleeping,
People: that awake we may watch with Christ, and asleep we may rest in peace.

Leader: May the divine help remain with us always.
People: And with those who are absent with us.

The Song of Simeon

This is the traditional canticle, the *Nunc Dimittus*, that is sung at this time.

Blessing

May the God of hope
> fill you with all joy and peace in believing,

so that you may abound in hope
> by the power of the Holy Spirit.

The Peace

APPENDIX C
THE COVENANT RENEWAL SERVICE

The following prayers are essential to the Covenant Renewal Service. These could be incorporated into a typical service that is usually done, or they could be used in a service unique for the congregation. These unique settings could be New Year's Eve (typically when it is celebrated as a Watch Night Service), Epiphany, or sometime during Lent. Charles Wesley wrote the hymn "Come, Let Us Use the Grace Divine" specifically for the opening of this service. This version of Wesley's Covenant Service is from the *United Methodist Book of Worship*. It is suggested that at least this portion of the service be available in written form for the congregation, along with a section for the members to sign and keep as a record of renewing their covenant with God.

Invitation

Leader:
>Commit yourselves to Christ as his servants.
>Give yourselves to him, that you may belong to him.
>Christ has many services to be done.
>Some are more easy and honorable,
>>others are more difficult and disgraceful.
>
>Some are suitable to our inclination and interests,
>>others are contrary to both.
>
>In some we may please Christ and please ourselves.
>But then there are other works where we cannot please Christ
>>except by denying ourselves.

It is necessary, therefore,
> that we consider what it means to be a servant of Christ.

Let us, therefore, go to Christ, and pray:

(Unison)

Let me be your servant, under your command.
I will no longer by my own.
I will give up myself to your will in all things.

Be satisfied that Christ shall give you your place and work.

Lord, make me what you will.
I put myself fully into your hands:
> **put me to doing, put me to suffering,**
> **let me be employed for you, or laid aside for you,**
> **let me be full, let me be empty,**
> **let me have all things, let me have nothing.**

I freely and with a willing heart
> **give it all to your pleasure and disposal.**

Christ will be the Savior of none but his servants.
He is the source of all salvation to those who obey.
Christ will have no servants except by consent;
Christ will not accept anything except full consent
> To all that he requires.

Christ will be all in all, or he will be nothing.

Confirm this by a holy covenant.

To make this covenant a reality in your life, listen to these admonitions:

First, set apart some time, more than once,
> to be spent alone before the Lord;
in seeking earnestly God's special assistance
> and gracious acceptance of you;
in carefully thinking through all the conditions of the covenant;
in searching your hearts

whether you have already freely given your life to Christ.
Consider what your sins are.
Consider the laws of Christ, how holy, strict, and spiritual they are,
>and whether you, after having carefully considered them,
>are willing to choose them all.
Be sure you are clear in these matters, see that you do not lie to God.

Second, be serious and in a spirit of holy awe and reverence.

Third, claim God's covenant,
rely upon God's promise of giving grace and strength,
>so you can keep your promise.
Trust not your own strength and power.

Fourth, resolve to be faithful.
You have given to the Lord your hearts,
>you have opened your mouths to the Lord,
>and you have dedicated yourself to God.
With God's power, never go back.

And last, be then prepared to renew your covenant with the Lord.
Fall down on your knees, lift your hands toward heaven,
>open your hearts to the Lord, as we pray:

Covenant Prayer

(Kneel or bow)

O righteous God, for the sake of your Son Jesus Christ,
>see me as I fall down before you.
Forgive my unfaithfulness in not having done your will,
>for you have promised mercy to me
>if I turn to you with my whole heart.

God requires that you shall put away all your idols.

I here from the bottom of my heart renounce them all,
>covenanting with you that no known sin shall be allowed
>in my life.

Against your will, I have turned my love toward the world.
In your power
    I will watch all temptations that will lead me away from you.
For my own righteousness is riddled with sin,
    unable to stand before you.

Through Christ, God has offered to be your God again
    if you would let him.

Before all heaven and earth,
    I here acknowledge you as my Lord and God.
I take you, Father, Son, and Holy Spirit, for my portion,
    and vow to give up myself, body and soul, as your servant,
    to serve you in holiness and righteousness all the days of my life.

God has given the Lord Jesus Christ
    as the only way and means of coming to God.

Jesus, I do here on bended knees accept Christ
    as the only new and living Way,
    and sincerely join myself in a covenant with him.
O blessed Jesus, I come to you,
    hungry, sinful, miserable, blind, and naked,
    unworthy even to wash the feet of your servants.
I do here, with all my power, accept you as my Lord and Head.
I renounce my own worthiness,
    and vow that you are the Lord, my righteousness.
I renounce my own wisdom, and take you for my only guide.
I renounce my own will, and take your will as my law.

Christ has told you that you must suffer with him.

I do here covenant with you, O Christ,
    to take my lot with you as it may fall.
Through your grace I promise
    that neither life nor death shall part me from you.

God has given holy laws as the rule of your life.

I do here willingly put my neck under your yoke, to carry your burden.

All your laws are holy, just, and good.

I therefore take them as the rule for my words, thoughts, and actions,
promising that I will strive
to order my whole life according to your direction,
and not allow myself to neglect anything I know to be my duty.

The almighty God searches and knows your heart.

O God, you know that I make this covenant with you today
without guile or reservation.

If any falsehood should be in it, guide me and help me to set it aright.

And now, glory be to you, O God the Father,
whom I from this day forward shall look upon as my God and Father.

Glory be to you, O God the Son,
who have loved me and washed me from my sins in your own blood,
and now is my Savior and Redeemer.

Glory be to you, O God the Holy Spirit,
who by your almighty power have turned my heart from sin to God.

O mighty God, the Lord Omnipotent, Father, Son, and Holy Spirit,
You have now become my Covenant Friend.

And I, through your infinite grace,
have become your covenant servant.

So be it.

And let the covenant I have made on earth be ratified in heaven.

Amen.

APPENDIX D
LECTIONARY

The Revised Common Lectionary is divided into a three-year cycle for the readings. Some days throughout the year have the same readings irrespective of the cycle year. Each year begins with the Advent readings, so whatever calendar year it is for Advent, the cycle year for the readings is dated from that. This means that the majority of the readings for calendar year 2020 will be on the cycle that has Advent in 2019.

For congregations that wish to use the lectionary, a few words of instruction may be helpful. If the congregation moves to using the lectionary from not using it, it will be necessary to explain to the entire body the reason behind the desire to use it as a tool and the fact that the scripture passages are already chosen for every Sunday. It may be beneficial to print the following week's readings in advance so the congregation will have time before the service to read and study scripture, should they so choose. In addition, it may be best to introduce only some of the readings in a particular service, especially if the congregation is not used to much scripture in a service. In that case, one potential would be to include the New Testament reading and the Gospel reading. After the congregation is used to multiple readings, the Psalm (which is typically a responsive reading between a leader and the congregation) can be introduced, with the Old Testament reading finally being added. On the other hand, sometimes it is best to make the full change all at once if the goal is to use all of the readings for a given Sunday. The case could be made to introduce all four readings

APPENDIX D

at once. The determining factor in either of these two scenarios is the personalities involved in the congregation and the leadership.

Most typically, if all of the readings are done, the Old Testament reading would come first. After it would be the Psalm reading, done as a responsive reading back and forth. Then the New Testament reading will occur. Finally, the Gospel reading is done. When there is more than one reading, people are usually asked to stand for the reading of the Gospel. The sermon follows the Gospel reading. One of the pitfalls of many preachers upon first using multiple readings from the lectionary is trying to tie in all of the readings to the message. There are some Sundays, Advent and Lent most specifically, in which this can happen. The connections between the readings are very obvious. There are other Sundays in which there is no thematic connection at all. The Old Testament readings and the New Testament readings tend to work through books without reference to the Gospel reading. In those cases, the sermon should be focused upon one of the readings for that day rather than trying to incorporate all of them into a message. The point of having scripture in a service is not just so it can be explained in a sermon; it is to expose people to scripture. In much of the American context today, Bibles are prevalent, yet Bible reading is almost nonexistent. Worship services become one place where people can actually hear portions of scripture.

	YEAR A	YEAR B	YEAR C	LITURGICAL COLOR
	2019, 2022, 2025	2020, 2023, 2026	2021, 2024, 2027	
1st Sunday of Advent	Is 2:1-5 Ps 122 Rom 13:11-14 Mt 24:36-44	Is 64:1-9 Ps 80:1-7, 17-19 1 Cor 1:3-9 Mk 13:24-37	Jer 33:14-16 Ps 25:1-10 1 Thess 3:9-13 Lk 21:25-36	Purple/Blue
2nd Sunday of Advent	Is 11:1-10 Ps 72:1-7, 18-19 Rom 15:4-13 Mt 3:1-12	Is 40:1-11 Ps 85:1-2, 8-13 2 Pet 3:8-15a Mk 1:1-8	Mal 3:1-4 Lk 1:68-79 Phil 1:3-11 Lk 3:1-6	Purple/Blue

APPENDIX D

	YEAR A	YEAR B	YEAR C	LITURGICAL COLOR
	2019, 2022, 2025	2020, 2023, 2026	2021, 2024, 2027	
3rd Sunday of Advent	Is 35:1-10 Ps 146:5-10 or Lk 1:46b-55 Jas 5:7-10 Mt 11:2-11	Is 61:1-4, 8-11 Ps 126 1 Thess 5:16-24 Jn 1:6-8, 19-28	Zeph 3:14-20 Is 12:2-6 Phil 4:4-7 Lk 3:7-18	Purple/Blue
4th Sunday of Advent	Is 7:10-16 Ps 80:1-7, 17-19 Rom 1:1-7 Mt 1:18-25	2 Sam 7:1-11, 16 Lk 1:47-55 Rom 16:25-27 Lk 1:26-38	Mic 5:2-5a Lk 1:47-55 Heb 10:5-10 Lk 1:39-45	Purple/Blue
Christmas Eve		Is 9:2-7 Ps 96 Titus 2:11-14 Lk 2:1-20		White
Christmas Day		Is 52:7-10 Ps 98 Heb 1:1-4 (5-12) Jn 1:1-14		White
First Sunday after Christmas	Is 63:7-9 Ps 148 Heb 2:10-18 Mt 2:13-23	Is 61:10–62:3 Ps 148 Gal 4:4-7 Lk 2:22-40	1 Sam 2:18-20, 26 Ps 148 Col 3:12-17 Lk 2:41-52	White
January 1		Eccl 3:1-13 Ps 8 Rev 21:1-6a Mt 25:31-46		White
Epiphany of the Lord (Jan. 6 or 1st Sunday of January)		Is 60:1-6 Ps 72:1-7, 10-14 Eph 3:1-12 Mt 2:1-12		White
Baptism of the Lord (Jan. 7–13, inclusive)	Is 42:1-9 Ps 29 Acts 10:34-43 Mt 3:13-17	Gen 1:1-5 Ps 29 Acts 19:1-7 Mk 1:4-11	Is 43:1-7 Ps 29 Acts 8:14-17 Lk 3:15-17, 21-22	White
Second Sunday after Epiphany (Jan. 14–20, inclusive)	Is 49:1-7 Ps 40:1-11 1 Cor 1:1-9 Jn 1:29-42	1 Sam 3:1-10 (11-20) Ps 139:1-6, 13,-18 1 Cor 6:12-20 Jn 1:43-51	Is 62:1-5 Ps 36:5-10 1 Cor 12:1-11 Jn 2:1-11	Green

APPENDIX D

	YEAR A	YEAR B	YEAR C	LITURGICAL COLOR
	2019, 2022, 2025	2020, 2023, 2026	2021, 2024, 2027	
Third Sunday after Epiphany (Jan. 21–27, inclusive)	Is 9:1-4 Ps 27:1, 4-9 1 Cor 1:10-18 Mt 4:12-23	Jonah 3:1-5, 10 Ps 62:5-12 1 Cor 7:29-31 Mk 1:14-20	Neh 8:1-3, 5-6, 8-10 Ps 19 1 Cor 12:12-31a Lk 4:14-21	Green
Fourth Sunday after Epiphany (Jan. 28–Feb.3, inclusive) (if last Sunday after Epiphany, see Transfiguration Sunday)	Mic 6:1-8 Ps 15 1 Cor 1:18-31 Mt 5:1-12	Deut 18:15-20 Ps 111 1 Cor 8:1-13 Mk 1:21-28	Jer 1:4-10 Ps 71:1-6 1 Cor 13:1-13 Lk 4:21-30	Green
Fifth Sunday after Epiphany (Feb. 4–10, inclusive) (if last Sunday after Epiphany, see Transfiguration Sunday)	Is 58:1-9a (9b-12) Ps 112:1-10 1 Cor 2:1-12 (13-16) Mt 5:13-20	Is 40:21-31 Ps 147:1-11, 20c 1 Cor 9:16-23 Mk 1:29-39	Is 6:1-8 (9-13) Ps 138 1 Cor 15:1-11 Lk 5:1-11	Green
Sixth Sunday after Epiphany (Feb. 11–17, inclusive) (if last Sunday after Epiphany, see Transfiguration Sunday)	Deut 30:15-20 Ps 119:1-8 1 Cor 3:1-9 Mt 5:21-37	2 Kings 5:1-14 Ps 30 1 Cor 9:24-27 Mk 1:40-45	Jer 17:5-10 Ps 1 1 Cor 15:12-20 Lk 6:17-26	Green
Seventh Sunday after Epiphany (Feb. 18–24, inclusive) (if last Sunday after Epiphany, see Transfiguration Sunday)	Lev 19:1-2, 9-18 Ps 119:33-40 1 Cor 3:10-11, 16-23 Mt 5:38-48	Is 43:18-25 Ps 41 2 Cor 1:18-22 Mk 2:1-12	Gen 45:3-11, 15 Ps 37:1-11, 39-40 1 Cor 15:35-38, 42-50 Lk 6:27-38	Green
Eighth Sunday after Epiphany (Feb. 25–29, inclusive) (if last Sunday after Epiphany, see Transfiguration Sunday)	Is 49:8-16a Ps 131 1 Cor 4:1-5 Mt 6:24-34	Hos 2:14-20 Ps 103:1-13, 22 2 Cor 3:1-6 Mk 2:13-22	Is 55:10-13 Ps 92:1-4, 12-15 1 Cor 15:51-58 Lk 6:39-49	Green

APPENDIX D

	YEAR A	YEAR B	YEAR C	LITURGICAL COLOR
	2019, 2022, 2025	2020, 2023, 2026	2021, 2024, 2027	
Transfiguration Sunday (Last Sunday after Epiphany)	Ex 24:12-18 Ps 2 or 99 2 Pet 1:16-21 Mt 17:1-9	2 Kings 2:1-12 Ps 50:1-6 2 Cor 4:3-6 Mk 9:2-9	Ex 34:29-35 Ps 99 2 Cor 3:12–4:2 Lk 9:28-36	White
Ash Wednesday	Joel 2:1-2, 12-17 Ps 51:1-17 2 Cor 5:20b-6:10 Mt 6:1-6, 16-21			Purple
First Sunday in Lent	Gen 2:15-17; 3:1-7 Ps 32 Rom 5:12-19 Mt 4:1-11	Gen 9:8-17 Ps 25:1–10 1 Pet 3:18-22 Mk 1:9-15	Deut 26:1-11 Ps 91:1-2, 9-16 Rom 10:8b-13 Lk 4:1-13	Purple
Second Sunday in Lent	Gen 12:1-4a Ps 121 Rom 4:1-5, 13-17 Jn 3:1-17 or Mt 17:1-9	Gen 17:1-7, 15-16 Ps 22:23-31 Rom 4:13-25 Mk 8:31-38	Gen 15:1-12, 17-18 Ps 27 Phil 3:17–4:1 Lk 13:31-35	Purple
Third Sunday in Lent	Ex 17:1-7 Ps 95 Rom 5:1-11 Jn 4:5-42	Ex 20:1-17 Ps 19 1 Cor 1:18-25 Jn 2:13-22	Is 55:1-9 Ps 63:1-8 1 Cor 10:1-13 Lk 13:1-9	Purple
Fourth Sunday in Lent	1 Sam 16:1-13 Ps 23 Eph 5:8-14 Jn 9:1-41	Num 21:4-9 Ps 107:1-3, 17-22 Eph 2:1-10 Jn 3:14-21	Josh 5:9-12 Ps 32 2 Cor 5:16-21 Lk 15:1-3, 11b-32	Purple
Fifth Sunday in Lent	Ezek 37:1-14 Ps 130 Rom 8:6-11 Jn 11:1-45	Jer 31:31-34 Ps 51:1-12 Heb 5:5-10 Jn 12:20-33	Is 43:16-21 Ps 126 Phil 3:4b-14 Jn 12:1-8	Purple
Palm/Passion Sunday	Palms Mt 21:1-11 Ps 118:1-2, 19-29 Passion Is 50:4-9a Ps 31:9-16 Phil 2:5-11 Mt 26:14–27:66 or Mt 27:11-54	Palms Mk 11:1-11 Ps 118:1-2, 19-29 Passion Is 50:4-9a Ps 31:9-16 Phil 2:5-11 Mk 14:1–15:47 or Mk 15:1-39 (40-47)	Palms Lk 19:28-40 Ps 118:1-2, 19-29 Passion Is 50:4-9a Ps 31:9-16 Phil 2:5-11 Lk 22:14–23:56 or Lk 23:1-49	Purple

APPENDIX D

	YEAR A 2019, 2022, 2025	YEAR B 2020, 2023, 2026	YEAR C 2021, 2024, 2027	LITURGICAL COLOR
Monday of Holy Week		Is 42:1-9 Ps 36:5-11 Heb 9:11-15 Jn 12:1-11		Purple
Tuesday of Holy Week		Is 49:1-7 Ps 71:1-14 1 Cor 1:18-31 Jn 12:20-36		Purple
Wednesday of Holy Week		Is 50:4-9a Ps 70 Heb 12:1-3 Jn 13:21-32		Purple
Holy/Maundy Thursday		Ex 12:1-4 (5-10) 11-14 Ps 116:1-4, 12-19 1 Cor 11:23-26 Jn 13:1-7, 31b-35		Purple
Good Friday		Is 52:13–53:12 Ps 22 Heb 10:16-25 Jn 18:1-19:42		Black
Easter Vigil*	Mt 28:1-10	Mk 16:1-8	Lk 24:1-12	White
Easter Day	Acts 10:34-43 Ps 118:1-2, 14-24 Col 3:1-4 Jn 20:1-18 or Mt 28:1-10	Acts 10:34-43 Ps 118:1-2, 14-24 1 Cor 15:1-11 Jn 20:1-18 or Mk 16:1-8	Acts 10:34-43 Ps 118:1-2, 14-24 1 Cor 15:19-26 Jn 20:1-18 or Lk 24:1-12	White
Second Sunday of Easter	Acts 2:14a, 22-32 Ps 16 1 Pet 1:3-9 Jn 20:19-31	Acts 4:32-35 Ps 133 1 Jn 1:1–2:2 Jn 20:19-31	Acts 5:27-32 Ps 150 Rev 1:4-8 Jn 20:19-31	White
Third Sunday of Easter	Acts 2:14a, 36-41 Ps 116:1-4, 12-19 1 Pet 1:17-23 Lk 24:13-35	Acts 3:12-19 Ps 4 1 Jn 3:1-7 Lk 24:36b-48	Acts 9:1-6 (7-20) Ps 30 Rev 5:11-14 Jn 21:1-19	White

APPENDIX D

	YEAR A	YEAR B	YEAR C	LITURGICAL COLOR
	2019, 2022, 2025	2020, 2023, 2026	2021, 2024, 2027	
Fourth Sunday of Easter	Acts 2:42-47 Ps 23 1 Pet 2:19-25 Jn 10:1-10	Acts 4:5-12 Ps 23 1 Jn 3:16-24 Jn 10:11-18	Acts 9:36-43 Ps 23 Rev 7:9-17 Jn 10:22-30	White
Fifth Sunday of Easter	Acts 7:55-60 Ps 31:1-5, 15-16 1 Pet 2:2-10 Jn 14:1-14	Acts 8:26-40 Ps 22:25-31 1 Jn 4:7-21 Jn 15:1-8	Acts 11:1-18 Ps 148 Rev 21:1-6 Jn 10:22-30	White
Sixth Sunday of Easter	Acts 17:22-31 Ps 66:8-20 1 Pet 3:13-22 Jn 14:15-21	Acts 10:44-48 Ps 98 1 Jn 5:1-6 Jn 15:9-17	Acts 16:9-15 Ps 67 Rev 21:10, 22-22:5 Jn 14:23-29	White
Ascension of the Lord (May be used for Seventh Sunday of Easter)		Acts 1:1-11 Ps 47 Eph 1:15-23 Lk 24:44-53		White
Seventh Sunday of Easter	Acts 1:6-14 Ps 68:1-10, 32-35 1 Pet 4:12-14; 5:6-11 Jn 17:1-11	Acts 1:15-17, 21-26 Ps 1 1 Jn 5:9-13 Jn 17:6-19	Acts 16:16-34 Ps 97 Rev 22:12-14, 16-17, 20-21 Jn 17:20-26	White
Pentecost	Acts 2:1-21 Ps 104:24-34, 35b 1 Cor 12:3b-13 Jn 7:37-39	Acts 2:1-21 Ps 104:24-34, 35b Rom 8:22-27 Jn 15:26-27; 16:4b-15	Acts 2:1-21 Ps 104:24-34, 35b Rom 8:14-17 Jn 14:8-17 (25-27)	Red
Trinity Sunday	Gen 1:1–2:4a Ps 8 2 Cor 13:11-13 Mt 28:16-20	Is 6:1-8 Ps 29 Rom 8:12-17 Jn 3:1-17	Prov 8:1-4, 22-31 Ps 8 Rom 5:1-5 Jn 16:12-15	White/Red

APPENDIX D

	YEAR A	YEAR B	YEAR C	LITURGICAL COLOR
	2019, 2022, 2025	2020, 2023, 2026	2021, 2024, 2027	
Sunday between May 29–June 4, inclusive (If after Trinity Sunday)	Gen 6:11-22; 7:24; 8:14-19 Ps 46 Rom 1:16-17; 3:22b-28 (29-31) Mt 7:21-29	1 Sam 3:1-20 Ps 139:1-6, 13-18 2 Cor 4:5-12 Mk 2:23-3:6	1 Kings 18:20-39 Ps 96 Gal 1:1-12 Lk 7:1-10	Green
Sunday between June 5–11, inclusive (If after Trinity Sunday)	Gen 12:1-9 Ps 33:1-12 Rom 4:13-25 Mt 9:9-13, 18-26	1 Sam 8:4-20 (11:14-15) Ps 138 2 Cor 4:13–5:1 Mk 3:20-35	1 Kings 17:8-24 Ps 146 Gal 1:11-24 Lk 7:11-17	Green
Sunday between June 12–18, inclusive (If after Trinity Sunday)	Gen 18:1-15 Ps 116:1-2, 12-19 Rom 5:1-8 Mt 9:35–10:8 (9-23)	1 Sam 15:34–16:13 Ps 20 or Ps 72 2 Cor 5:6-10 (11-13), 14-17 Mk 4:26-34	1 Kings 21:1-21a Ps 5:1-8 Gal 2:15-21 Lk 7:36–8:3	Green
Sunday between June 19–25, inclusive (If after Trinity Sunday)	Gen 21:8-21 Ps 86:1-10, 16-17 or Ps 17 Rom 6:1b-11 Mt 10:24-39	1 Sam 17:(1a, 4-11, 19-23) 32-49 Ps 9:9-20 2 Cor 6:1-13 Mk 4:35-41	1 Kings 19:1-15a Ps 42 Gal 3:23-29 Lk 8:26-39	Green
Sunday between June 26–July 2, inclusive	Gen 22:1-14 Ps 13 Rom 6:12-23 Mt 10:40-42	2 Sam 1:1, 17-27 Ps 130 2 Cor 8:7-15 Mk 5:21-43	2 Kings 2:1-2, 6-14 Ps 77:1-2, 11-20 Gal 5:1, 13-25 Lk 9:51-62	Green
Sunday between July 3–9, inclusive	Gen 24:34-38, 42-49, 58-67 Ps 45:10-17 or Ps 72 Rom 7:15-25a Mt 11:16-19, 25-30	2 Sam 5:1-5, 9-10 Ps 48 2 Cor 12:2-10 Mk 6:1-13	2 Kings 5:1-14 Ps 30 Gal 6:(1-6) 7-16 Lk 10:1-11, 16-20	Green

APPENDIX D

	YEAR A 2019, 2022, 2025	YEAR B 2020, 2023, 2026	YEAR C 2021, 2024, 2027	LITURGICAL COLOR
Sunday between July 10–16, inclusive	Gen 25:19-34 Ps 119:105-112 or Ps 25 Rom 8:1-11 Mt 13:1-9, 18-23	2 Sam 6:1-5, 12b-19 Ps 24 Eph 1:3-14 Mk 6:14-29	Amos 7:7-17 Ps 82 Col 1:1-14 Lk 10:25-37	Green
Sunday between July 17–23, inclusive	Gen 28:10-19a Ps 139:1-12, 23-24 Rom 8:12-25 Mt 13:24-30, 36-43	2 Sam 7:1-14a Ps 89:20-37 Eph 2:11-22 Mk 6:30-34, 53-56	Amos 8:1-12 Ps 52 or Ps 82 Col 1:15-28 Lk 10:38-42	Green
Sunday between July 24–30, inclusive	Gen 29:15-28 Ps 105:1-11, 45b Rom 8:26-39 Mt 13:31-33, 44-52	2 Sam 11:1-15 Ps 14 Eph 3:14-21 Jn 6:1-21	Hos 1:2-10 Ps 85 Col 2:6-15 (16-19) Lk 11:1-13	Green
Sunday between July 31–Aug. 6, inclusive	Gen 32:22-31 Ps 17:1-7, 15 Rom 9:1-5 Mt 14:13-21	2 Sam 11:26–12:13a Ps 51:1-12 Eph 4:1-16 Jn 6:24-35	Hos 11:1-11 Ps 107:1-9, 43 Col 3:1-11 Lk 12:13-21	Green
Sunday between Aug. 7–13, inclusive	Gen 37:1-4, 12-28 Ps 105:1-6, 16-22, 45b Rom 10:5-15 Mt 14:22-33	2 Sam 18:5-9, 15, 31-33 Ps 130 Eph 4:25–5:2 Jn 6:35, 41-51	Is 1:1, 10-20 Ps 50:1-8, 22-23 Heb 11:1-3, 8-16 Lk 12:32-40	Green
Sunday between Aug. 14–20, inclusive	Gen 45:1-15 Ps 133 Rom 11:1-2a, 29-32 Mt 15:(10-20) 21-28	1 Kings 2:10-12; 3:3-14 Ps 111 Eph 5:15-20 Jn 6:51-58	Is 5:1-7 Ps 80:1-2, 8-19 Heb 11:29–12:2 Lk 12:49-56	Green
Sunday between Aug. 21–27, inclusive	Ex 1:8-2:10 Ps 124 Rom 12:1-8 Mt 16:13-20	1 Kings 8:(1, 6, 10-11) 22-30, 41-43 Ps 84 Eph 6:10-20 Jn 6:56-69	Jer 1:4-10 Ps 71:1-6 Heb 12:18-29 Lk 13:10-17	Green

APPENDIX D

	YEAR A	YEAR B	YEAR C	LITURGICAL COLOR
	2019, 2022, 2025	2020, 2023, 2026	2021, 2024, 2027	
Sunday between Aug. 28–Sept. 3, inclusive	Ex 3:1-15 Ps 105:1-6, 23-26, 45c Rom 12:9-21 Mt 16:21-28	Song 2:8-13 Ps 45:1-2, 6-9 or Ps 72 Jas 1:17-27 Mk 7:1-8, 14-15, 21-23	Jer 2:4-13 Ps 81:1, 10-16 Heb 13:1-8, 15-16 Lk 14:1, 7-14	Green
Sunday between Sept. 4–10, inclusive	Ex 12:1-14 Ps 149 or Ps 148 Rom 13:8-14 Mt 18:15-20	Prov 22:1-2, 8-9, 22-23 Ps 125 or Ps 124 Jas 2:1-10 (11-13), 14-17 Mk 7:24-37	Jer 18:1-11 Ps 139:1-6, 13-18 Philem 1-21 Lk 14:25-33	Green
Sunday between Sept. 11–17, inclusive	Ex 14:19-31 Ex 15:1b-11, 20-21 Rom 14:1-12 Mt 18:21-35	Prov 1:20-33 Ps 19 Jas 3:1-12 Mk 8:27-38	Jer 4:11-12, 22-28 Ps 14 1 Tim 1:12-17 Lk 15:1-10	Green
Sunday between Sept. 18–24, inclusive	Ex 16:2-15 Ps 105:1-6, 37-45 or Ps 78 Phil 1:21-30 Mt 20:1-16	Prov 31:10-31 Ps 1 Jas 3:13–4:3, 7-8a Mk 9:30-37	Jer 8:18–9:1 Ps 79:1-9 or Ps 4 1 Tim 2:1-7 Lk 16:1-13	Green
Sunday between Sept. 25–Oct. 1, inclusive	Ex 17:1-7 Ps 78:1-4, 12-16 Phil 2:1-13 Mt 21:23-32	Esth 7:1-6, 9-10; 9:20-22 Ps 124 Jas 5:13-20 Mk 9:38-50	Jer 32:1-3a, 6-15 Ps 91:1-6, 14-16 1 Tim 6:6-19 Lk 16:19-31	Green
Sunday between Oct. 2–8, inclusive	Ex 20:1-4, 7-9, 12-20 Ps 19 Phil 3:4b-14 Mt 21:33-46	Job 1:1, 2:1-10 Ps 26 or Ps 25 Heb 1:1-4; 2:5-12 Mk 10:2-16	Lam 1:1-6 Ps 137 2 Tim 1:1-14 Lk 17:5-10	Green
Sunday between Oct. 9–15, inclusive	Ex 32:1-14 Ps 106:1-6, 19-23 Phil 4:1-9 Mt 22:1-14	Job 23:1-9, 16-17 Ps 22:1-15 Heb 4:12-16 Mk 10:17-31	Jer 29:1, 4-7 Ps 66:1-12 2 Tim 2:8-15 Lk 17:11-19	Green

APPENDIX D

	YEAR A	YEAR B	YEAR C	LITURGICAL COLOR
	2019, 2022, 2025	2020, 2023, 2026	2021, 2024, 2027	
Sunday between Oct. 16–22, inclusive	Ex 33:1-12 Ps 99 1 Thess 2:1-8 Mt 22:34-46	Job 38:1-7 (34-41) Ps 104:1-9, 24, 35c Heb 5:1-10 Mk 10:35-45	Jer 31:27-34 Ps 119:97-104 or Ps 19 2 Tim 3:14–4:5 Lk 18:1-8	Green
Sunday between Oct. 23–29, inclusive	Deut 34:1-12 Ps 90:1-6, 13-17 1 Thess 2:1-8 Mt 22:34-46	Job 42:1-6, 10-17 Ps 34:1-8 (19-22) Heb 7:23-28 Mk 10:46-52	Joel 2:23-32 Ps 65 2 Tim 4:6-8, 16-18 Lk 18:9-14	Green
Sunday between Oct. 30–Nov. 5, inclusive	Josh 3:7-17 Ps 107:1-7, 33-37 1 Thess 2:9-13 Mt 23:1-12	Ruth 1:1-18 Ps 146 Heb 9:11-14 Mk 12:28-34	Hab 1:1-4; 2:1-4 Ps 119:137-144 2 Thess 1:1-4, 11-12 Lk 19:1-10	Green
All Saints Day (Nov. 1 or 1st Sunday in Nov.)	Rev 7:9-17 Ps 34:1-10, 22 1 Jn 3:1-3 Mt 5:1-12	Is 25:6-9 Ps 24 Rev 21:1-6a Jn 11:32-44	Dan 7:1-3, 15-18 Ps 149 or Ps 150 Eph 1:11-23 Lk 6:20-31	Green
Sunday between Nov. 6–12, inclusive	Josh 24:1-3a, 14-25 Ps 78:1-7 1 Thess 4:13-18 Mt 25:1-13	Ruth 3:1-5; 4:13-17 Ps 127 or Ps 42 Heb 9:24-28 Mk 12:38-44	Hag 1:15b–2:9 Ps 145:1-5, 17-21 2 Thess 2:1-5, 13-17 Lk 20:27-38	Green
Sunday between Nov. 13–19, inclusive	Judg 4:1-7 Ps 123 or Ps 76 1 Thess 5:1-11 Mt 25:14-30	1 Sam 1:4-20 1 Sam 2:1-10 or Ps 113 Heb 10:11-14 (15-18) 19-25 Mk 13:1-8	Is 65:17-25 Is 12 or Ps 118 2 Thess 3:6-13 Lk 21:5-19	Green
Reign of Christ (Nov. 20–26, inclusive)	Ezek 34:11-16, 20-24 Ps 100 Eph 1:15-23 Mt 25:31-46	2 Sam 23:1-7 Ps 132:1-12 Rev 1:4b-8 Jn 18:33-37	Jer 23:1-6 Lk 1:68-79 Col 1:11-20 Lk 23:33-43	White

APPENDIX D

	YEAR A	YEAR B	YEAR C	LITURGICAL COLOR
	2019, 2022, 2025	2020, 2023, 2026	2021, 2024, 2027	
Thanksgiving Day	Deut 8:7-18 Ps 65 2 Cor 9:6-15 Lk 17:11-19	Joel 2:21-27 Ps 126 1 Tim 2:1-7 Mt 6:25-33	Deut 26:1-11 Ps 100 Phil 4:4-9 Jn 6:25-35	Green

*The Easter Vigil service has numerous Old Testament readings. The amount of readings is not prescribed; however, one of them should be from Exodus 14. The Gospel readings change depending upon which cycle of readings are in which year (A, B, or C), but the following readings are for all three years:

Gen 1:1–2:4a
Ps 136:1-9, 23-26 or Ps 33

Gen 7:1-5, 11-18; 8:6-18; 9:8-13
Ps 46

Gen 22:1-18
Ps 16

Ex 14:10-31; 15:20-21
Ex 15:1b-13, 17-18

Is 55:1-11
Is 12:2-6

Ezek 36:24-28
Ps 42

Ezek 37:1-14
Ps 43

Rom 6:3-11
Ps 114

INDEX

advent, 100–5, 217–19

altar-table, 19, 52–55, 61, 103, 181–83

Anglican Church, 37–40, 105, 115, 127n, 193

Apostolic Constitutions, 87–90

baptism, infant, 121–27

Book of Common Prayer, 38, 171, 203

calendar, 106–8

Calvin, John, 152, 162

canticles, 158–59, 162

chancel, 52–53, 60–61, 182, 183, 190

Christmas, season, 100–106

colors, liturgical, 103–5, 189

communion table, 181–83. See also altar-table

confirmation, 34, 86, 104, 126–27

consubstantiation, 151

Didache, 16–17, 29, 31, 33, 131

Divine Liturgy, 8, 91–95

Dura-Europos, 50–51, 58, 115, 132, 184

Eastern Orthodox, 8, 54, 56, 91–95, 126, 134, 145, 147, 148, 150, 191, 193

Easter Season, 100–6, 109, 188–89

epiclesis, 59

Epiphany, 100–102, 211

Holy week, 101

hours, liturgical, 7, 170–71

hymnal, 162–65

Ignatius of Antioch, 18–20, 31–33, 149

incense, 60, 187–88, 206–7

Irenaeus, 32–33, 149

Justin Martyr, 21–25, 85–86, 89–90, 149, 150, 183

lectionaries, 108–11, 190

lent, 100–105, 109, 188–89, 211

Luther, Martin, 108, 148, 151–52, 161–62

Mass, 8, 26, 54-55, 91–95, 151

memorialism, 145, 148, 151

Methodists, 8, 10, 30, 105, 127, 128–30, 136, 137, 140, 148, 153, 162, 175–79, 196–97; open table practice, 154–55; order of worship, 9–96; ordination, 25–26, 37–42, 45–47. *See also* Wesley, Charles; Wesley, John

Ordinary time, 100, 104, 109
ordination of women, 42–45

paraments, 103
Pentecost, 71, 100, 102, 104, 132, 170, 182

Roman Catholic Church, 8, 30, 34–35, 41-42, 52–55, 61, 91–92, 103, 105, 109–10, 126–27, 134, 145–46, 148, 150–52, 191–93

sermon, 24, 60, 96, 97–98, 110, 166, 190
society meeting, 96–97

Tertullian, 123–24
transubstantiation, 150–52

vestments, 92, 105, 191–93
virtualism, 152

Wesley, Charles, 39-40, 108, 157–58, 162, 211
Wesley, John, 5, 38–40, 45–46, 96, 108, 115, 127, 135–36, 153, 171, 176, 178, 197

Zwingli, Ulrich, 148, 151–53, 161–62

BX
8337
.B78
2019